Faith-Building Stories for All Ages

INCREASE my FAITH

Maureen Huber

© April 2007 Carlisle Press

All rights reserved. No portion of this book may be reproduced by any means, electronic or mechanical, including photocopying, recording, or by any information storage retrieval system, without written permission of the copyright owner, except for the inclusion of brief quotations for a review.

ISBN 10-digit: 1-933753-04-8
ISBN 13-digit: 9-781933-753041

Text and cover design: Teresa Hochstetler
Cover art: Mahlon Troyer © 2006 Marcus Wengerd Art Collection
Printed by: Carlisle Printing

Carlisle Press
WALNUT CREEK

2673 Twp. Rd. 421
Sugarcreek, OH 44681

Introduction

WE MAKE CHOICES IN life with the chronicles of history in our favor. The things we have learned influence the way we act and feel, the way we speak and decide, and the way we believe. Across the panorama of two thousand years of proof, we gaze backward to the Empty Tomb and judge the matters pertaining to our faith.

Yet our confidence still falters at times as hope dims and determination wavers, and men and women who have known the feel of Everest beneath their feet sink to the abyss of despair and brush close by the very gates of hell. Sometimes the glow of the encounter with the Divine has scarce paled from the face of the worshiper when, behind his back, the tempter glides in softly and feathers away with one shred of doubt the bits of rose-colored dust he had mistaken for mountain-moving faith.

Mindful, then, of the fragility of the faith we experience this side of Golgotha, we ought to be the more amazed at the commitment shown by the saints of the Old Testament. For they, looking forward through the veil of history yet to be written, steadfastly grounded their faith upon the prophesied truths we have the privilege of viewing as facts.

This confidence they had in God—this faith in the absence of proof—can, if we allow it to, inspire us to set our feet more firmly upon the hills of triumph. Then, in the light of their confidence and the knowledge of their victory, we can with joyous anticipation and holy wonder pray, "Lord, increase my faith!"

—*Maureen Huber*

Contents

Don't Let Him Go! 1
Great-Grandmother's Job 7
No Good for Anything? 13
The Living Proof 21
Jessica or Lima Beans? 31
The Problem with Eric 35
Should I Confess? 39
All Such Desires 44
Twenty-seven Years 49
Walking on Coals 54
A Little Fun 61
Dilemma in Dutch 68
Beyond My Expectations 72
Love Will Make It Possible 78
Not Like Uncle Elwood! 83
From What I Heard 92
Did Carl Forget? 95
Peace on His Terms 98
I'd Give up Anything! 107

Don't Let Him Go!

"LET'S CONTINUE TO PRAY for Keith Levitt," Brother Jonathan suggested as the congregation shared their prayer burdens together on Wednesday evening. "We want him to find salvation again."

Tears sprang to Rachel Levitt's eyes at the minister's words. How faithful the congregation had been in praying for her wayward husband. Three long, lonely years had passed since she last saw him. How often she had wondered in those years what she could have done to prevent him from leaving. How might she have kept him from losing his way with the Lord?

She had sensed during the weeks before he left that he

was not his usual happy self. And she had been especially concerned about the unhealthy contacts he had been making with Joe Burskind. Joe and Keith had been close before Keith had become a Christian, but Rachel knew that now Joe's influence would have the wrong effect on her husband.

Then one morning in July, Keith failed to come for breakfast at his usual time. Nothing could have prepared Rachel for the note that she found on the cream separator when she went to the barn to look for him.

"I'm done keeping up the front," it read. "I'm tired of pretending. It's not working. If I ever find my way out of this mess, I'll come back."

That was all. He hadn't even told her that he loved her.

How clearly she remembered the nausea that washed over her as she sank onto a cream can close to the separator where he had left the message. "Keith. My Keith. Gone—perhaps forever. Please, oh please, Lord, bring my Keith back home!"

In the days and weeks that followed, the shock of his leaving gradually wore away. With five small children plus the farmwork to care for, Rachel was always busy—busy enough that she could not have done more. Again and again she committed herself and the children to God's care, and again and again she besought the Lord to draw her husband to Himself.

"I want to accept this as something You have chosen

to allow for me," she prayed. "I claim Your grace, Lord. Without it, I am nothing. Help me to raise our children to love and serve You."

But the loneliness, the heartache, the agony of knowing that her husband's soul was not safe in Jesus, always remained. Week after week and month after month for three years now she had prayed. Sometimes she was confident that God would answer soon. At other times she almost despaired.

The minister's voice went on to other things now, but Rachel did not hear. "Oh, Lord, You know how I desire to have Keith come home. But even more, I long to be sure that all is well with his soul."

Year after year continued to pass by, and the worn slip of paper with Keith's message grew frayed in Rachel's Bible. It was her last communication from him.

Was he still alive? "Lord, if he is, please draw him to Yourself. Speak to his heart and bring him back, Lord. Please don't let him go!"

Five years passed, then ten, and then fifteen. The children grew up, and one by one they got married. Still Rachel interceded. "Father, if only I could know that his soul is safe. Continue to draw him, Lord. Don't let him go, oh Father. Don't let him go to hell!"

Finally twenty years had come and gone. The children were all married now, and Rachel was enjoying her grandchildren. Whenever one of the children needed help, she would spend some time in that particular home.

Thus it was Rachel who answered when the phone rang one afternoon in her oldest son's home.

"Hello," the voice on the other end replied to her greeting. "This is Donald Reamer. Is Sister Rachel Levitt there, or can you tell me where I can contact her?"

Rachel was puzzled. Donald Reamer. She hardly knew him. He had been in the community as an evangelist once or perhaps twice in the past thirty years. Why would he want to speak to her now?

"This is Rachel," she said hesitantly. "Can I help you?"

"Sister Levitt." The evangelist's voice was gentle. "Perhaps you ought to sit down. I have some very unusual news for you."

Obediently Rachel sat on a nearby chair. "I'm sitting now," she said into the mouthpiece.

"Sister Levitt, I'm calling from New York City. During the past week, I've been holding revival meetings at the _____ Street Mission. They have a register at the back of the building where those who attend are encouraged to sign. Sometimes I look at it after the service.

"On Monday evening this week," he continued, "a man who appeared to be quite ill sat on the back bench in the auditorium. He wept all through the service. I was eager to talk with him, of course. But by the time I reached the back of the building, he had disappeared. I checked the register then, and found Keith Levitt's name."

Tears streamed down Rachel's cheeks as she listened in silence to the voice at the other end of the line.

"Oh, Brother Reamer! Do you think it could be my Keith? There might be another Keith Levitt, you know. New York City is big…" The words trailed off and Rachel mopped at her tears.

"I thought about that too," the evangelist admitted. "And I felt that I had to know. Since he was gone, however, I hardly knew where to begin.

"Yet I felt compelled to find him. I searched the area for two days without success. Then early this morning, while I was praying for guidance in locating him, the Lord reminded me that the man had appeared very ill. So I began to check the hospitals here in the city.

"Sister Levitt, your husband is in _____ ___ _____ Hospital here in New York City. He found the Lord Jesus as his personal Savior a few minutes ago, and now he wants to see you. He's critically ill. Can you come immediately? He keeps asking how soon we think you can be here."

For several moments Rachel fought to gain control of her emotions so that she could speak. "Of course I'll come," she managed to sob at last. "Tell Keith that I'm coming as fast as I can. And tell him I love him and forgive him," she added. "Tell him I've prayed for him every day for the twenty years he's been gone."

"I'll be waiting for you here whenever you arrive," the evangelist said. "I told Keith that I won't leave. He's in room 407. It's on the fourth floor of the northeast wing."

Rachel replaced the receiver and sank to her knees beside the chair on which she had been sitting. "Thank you, Father," she sobbed aloud. "Thank you that You didn't let him go!"

Rachel rested and prayed by turns throughout the following hours. Her two sons took turns sleeping and driving as they traveled toward the city. As the long hours crept toward morning, the aura of light from New York City appeared on the horizon.

"We'll be there before rush hour," Rachel said to her sons. To herself, she added, "Oh, Lord, if it is Your will, please let Keith live until I've talked to him. You know how desperately I want to tell him myself that I forgive him."

The June dawn was casting long shadows as the weary travelers crawled stiffly from their vehicle. Rachel's heart beat faster as she walked toward the hospital. Was Keith still alive? "May it be according to Your will, Lord," she prayed silently as her oldest son opened the door and stepped back for her to enter. The support of his arm about her brought fresh tears of gratitude as she stepped silently into the elevator.

A few minutes later, they saw Brother Reamer sitting on a chair beside a door that was numbered 407. His Bible was open on his lap.

"Sister Rachel, I'm glad you've arrived," he greeted

her. Rachel could tell by his expression that her husband was still alive.

Brother Reamer opened the door, and Rachel stepped into her husband's hospital room. There were four beds. The evangelist motioned toward the one in the farthest corner.

"Thank you, Father, thank you!" Rachel rejoiced as she moved silently toward it. She brushed her tears aside as she approached the wasted form of the sleeping man.

How cruel the years of sin had been! "But thank you, Father, that You saved his soul!" Trembling, she reached for the wrinkled hand that lay on top of the covers.

"Keith," she whispered softly as tears fell on his cheek. "Keith, Sweetheart, it's Rachel. I'm here."

The man on the bed stirred fretfully, then slowly opened his eyes.

"Rachel!" He caught her hand in a feeble grasp and brought it to his lips. "Rachel, I'm sorry. So sorry! And so very glad you've come."

Two hours later, as Rachel held his hands in hers, Keith drew his final breath.

"Thank you for answering my prayers, Lord," Rachel prayed as she laid the limp hands back onto the cover. "Thank you for saving his soul. Thank you that You didn't let him go!"

Great-Grandmother's Job

FATHER MILLER PUSHED HIS chair away from the kitchen table. "The way our work is shaping up," he said, "I think we'll be able to go to the Miller gathering next Saturday." He smiled at the exclamations of delight from his family.

"We'll plan to stay there for a few days, of course," he added. "It's a fifteen-hour drive, so we'll try to make the trip worthwhile."

Little tingles of anticipation ran over Lillian as she took in the news. The family gathering. She hadn't been to one since she was six. Often in the ten years since, their family had hoped to go, but each year something had come up that made it impossible, and they had put it off for another year.

Her younger sisters' chatter was lost on Lillian while

the three of them did the supper dishes. "Let me see," she mused. "I remember all Father's brothers and sisters and their companions. Of course they might not all be there. But my cousins, well, that will be different. I've not met some of them for many years, and most of the younger ones I've never met at all. And everyone will have changed in the years since I last saw them."

Then there would be Great-Grandmother. Lillian had not seen her since Father's youngest sister had married eight years ago. Great-Grandmother had not been well since that time, so the fifteen-hour trip to the area where Lillian's family lived had been too much for her to attempt. Father had gone with Grandfathers to visit her twice in that time, but Mother and the children had not been able to go along.

"Seeing Great-Grandmother will be the highlight of the trip," Lillian concluded now. "I'll have to get out the photo album and look up some of my cousins, though; I want to be able to recognize them too."

A few days later, the Millers were on their way. "Are we almost there, Mother?" four-year-old Joel inquired. Lillian smiled. It must have been at least the tenth time he had asked.

Mother shifted the sleeping toddler on her lap. "It will take just a few more minutes," she replied.

"You're ready to get out of this van and run, aren't you?" Lillian asked as she patted the fair head beside her on the back seat. "It's been a long ride."

Her little brother nodded eagerly. "And pretty soon I can!"

Lillian smiled at him fondly. Her own eager anticipation of the trip had been tempered somewhat during the days since Father's announcement that they would be going by the fact that there would be so many people she hardly knew and so many she did not know at all.

As they turned into Great-Uncle Earl's driveway, Lillian caught her breath at the sight of more than two hundred people scattered about the spacious lawn. She breathed a sigh of partial relief to know that at least there should not be more arriving after they did. They had forgotten about the time change until they were on the road, so they were an hour later than they had planned to be.

Father had called ahead when he realized what had happened, and Great-Uncle Earl had assured him that they would all wait to have lunch until the Millers arrived.

"We'll go and talk to Great-Grandmother while Uncle Earl finishes getting everybody organized for lunch," Father decided as the family got out of the van. "That way, she can see us all together."

Lillian knew a few of these people from previous acquaintance, and she had studied the family photo album enough to recognize a number of the individuals she had never met. But many of the people she saw now were just strange faces, in spite of the pictures she had studied so carefully.

"I'd hardly even remember Great-Grandmother without having seen her picture," she told Mother as they walked across the lawn toward the rocking chair that sat in the shade of a maple tree in the center of the lawn.

Father smiled as he bent over to shake hands with Great-Grandmother who was seated in the rocker.

"Why, it's Charles!" she exclaimed. "And Marion! You have your family along too. Well, isn't this nice? Let me see. How long is it since you were at a Miller gathering?"

"Ten years, I'm afraid," Father admitted. "We wanted to come every year, and several times we even made plans to. But each time something came up so that it didn't work. We're especially glad to be here this time now, and the children have been looking forward to it too."

Great-Grandmother shook hands with Mother then, and they chatted for a moment. Then she looked around upon the circle of seven children. "Let's see," she said slowly. "This is Lillian … and Richard … and Ruth … and Marcia … and Allen … and Joel … and Peter." She shook hands with them as she said their names.

"Lillian, you'll be sixteen for a while yet, won't you? And Richard will soon be fifteen. Ruth was twelve in February, and Marcia will be nine next month. Allen, you're six now, I believe, and Joel is almost four. And Peter will be two in a couple more months."

Lillian stood silent in open-mouthed wonder as Great-Grandmother went down the line, getting not only their names but also their ages right in every case. This dear old lady had sixty-seven grandchildren and well over a hundred great-grandchildren. Did she know them all like this—even the ones she had never met except through pictures? She certainly had never seen Marcia, Allen, Joel, or Peter!

Lillian glanced around, but no one was listening except her family, so she summoned up her courage and inquired, "Great-Grandmother, do you mind if I ask how you know all our names and ages? You've never even seen Marcia or Allen or Joel or Peter. And Richard and Ruth and I were little children when you saw us last. How can you remember our names and ages as you do?"

Great-Grandmother smiled gently. "That's a fair question, Lillian," she said. "The answer is easy enough. Ever since your great-grandfather died almost fifty years ago, I've tended to sleep very poorly. When I couldn't sleep, I'd pray for our children, and in the case of those who were married, for their companions. If I still couldn't sleep, I'd pray for their children. As the years went on, there were great-grandchildren too. When I still couldn't sleep, I'd pray for them as well.

"Time went on, of course," Great-Grandmother continued. "After a while, I couldn't work much anymore. So I guess I took up praying as my job. When you pray for someone every day, you feel as though you know them even if you've never actually seen them. And pictures help, of course. So does my little list of names and birthdays."

Lillian was glad that Great-Uncle Earl called for everyone's attention just then, so that she did not have to produce an acknowledgment to Great-Grandmother's answer to her question. A big lump had come from somewhere and stuck in her throat. How could she have managed to force words around it?

"So almost every day of my whole life—nearly seventeen years—Great-Grandmother has prayed for me!" Lillian was thankful that everyone had their eyes closed as she kept wiping away the tears that insisted on sliding down her cheeks. Meanwhile, a great-uncle she barely remembered gave thanks for their food.

"Thank you, Father," Lillian prayed simply. "Thank you for a great-grandmother like mine!"

Two more years passed, and Lillian did not find another opportunity to visit with Great-Grandmother. Then one day they received the phone call that she had come to dread. Great-Grandmother had died. A stroke. As unexpected as death can be when one is ninety-five.

How many times in the two years since she had last seen her, Lillian wondered now, had she remembered that Great-Grandmother prayed for her every day? How often had the knowledge given her courage to be faithful to the Lord and a good example to her younger brothers and sisters?

Lillian was mature enough now to realize that not only Great-Grandmother's prayers, but her knowledge of them, had had a profound effect on her life. But now

Great-Grandmother would pray for her no more.

Lillian tried to choke back her sobs as Father told them the content of the phone call. The tears came anyhow. She was glad for Great-Grandmother's sake that the Lord had chosen to take her home.

Her long night vigils of half a century were over now; her days of waiting done. The body would soon return to dust; the spirit was already with the Lord. Great-Grandmother was at rest, her labors complete.

"But what about me?" something inside of Lillian protested. "Who will take Great-Grandmother's place? Who will pray for me the way she did?" A great agony of spirit seemed almost to smother her as she realized that nobody ever would. Her great-grandmother would never be replaced.

"Heavenly Father," her heart cried out in agony, "help me to endure this terrible loss. Teach me to be submissive to Your plan. Make me, through this experience, closer to what You desire for me to be. I give Great-Grandmother up to You, Lord. I never deserved to have someone like her. Thank you for allowing her to pray for me for almost nineteen years!"

No Good for Anything?

———◆———

RAYMOND SIGHED AS HE bent to retrieve the sap pail that he had dropped. It was the third time this morning that he had fumbled one into the snow, and of course it was always the fullest buckets that spilled.

"I used to look forward to being out of school so I could really help with syrup making," he reflected. "And now this. Lord, I don't understand. Why? Why? Why? Syrup making used to be one of the highlights of the year."

No one knew when Raymond was younger that more was involved in his problem than simply slow muscle development. "Be patient," Father had encouraged many times. "You'll get stronger by and by. Meanwhile, let the other boys carry the fuller buckets."

But Raymond did not get stronger—not as quickly as other boys anyhow. The increasing strength and improving coordination of his friends seemed to mock his awkwardness and highlight his weakness.

Then came the trip to the specialist when Raymond was fourteen. The kind but serious face of the doctor came to his memory now. "Be satisfied to do what you can, Son. There's nothing that I or anyone can do to change your body. You have an incurable disease. But it doesn't affect your mind, and it won't likely affect your hands for many years. You'll have limitations, but you'll also have opportunities. You're tough—you'll learn to cope. It won't be easy, but I know you can do it!"

At nineteen now, Raymond knew that the doctor had been right. He never would get strong. He was getting weaker instead. Like old Mr. Davis at the nursing home where the young people went to sing, he would someday be a prisoner in his own body—a wild-born bird shut up in a cage with nothing but memories of the dew-soft air of an April morning, clean and exhilarating against its pulsing wings.

The day would come when he would be no good for anything. Just another burden for someone to bear. He turned to replace the empty bucket on the spile that stuck out from the hole he had drilled in the maple tree. His toe caught beneath a snow-covered root and he sprawled onto the ground.

The following morning at the breakfast table, his father announced that he thought they should visit Aunt Sally that evening.

"She's lonely, living all by herself," Father concluded. "We ought to go more often."

Mother nodded. "Should we call Wilburs and see if they'd like to go too? Then there would be enough of us to sing. Sally likes that so well."

Aunt Sally, Mother's widowed oldest sister, lived nearby. Wilbur was Raymond's oldest brother. He and his wife and family lived on the farm next to Raymond's parents' property.

"Our opportunities to sing for Sally aren't going to last forever either," Father added. "Since she has cancer now, she won't likely be here much longer."

"I wonder how long she'll be able to live alone." Mother didn't say more, but they knew what she was thinking. Aunt Sally would probably soon need constant care, and Mother would be the one who would provide it.

Aunt Sally had learned that she had cancer several months before. Her decision not to accept medical treatment had caused questions for some of her friends. But those who had stood by her when her husband suffered the miseries of cancer treatment a few years earlier felt that they understood why she refused.

Cancer, Raymond thought now. It sounded so final. Yet Aunt Sally was calm and very much at peace.

When supper was over that evening, they drove to her house.

"Come in! Come in!" she welcomed them. Her voice

quivered, but there was no lack of warmth in the invitation. "Never mind me," she went on. "I'll just get out of the way."

She swung herself deftly away from the door on her crutches. Aunt Sally had walked with crutches as long as Raymond could remember. He never gave them a thought. It was as though the sticks of wood were a part of his aunt.

The evening passed quickly, with visiting and singing, and Raymond was glad he had come. As they were about to leave, Father asked Aunt Sally whether she had any struggles now to accept the cancer verdict.

Aunt Sally shook her head. "It hasn't been a big adjustment," she said slowly. "Cancer is different, of course. Maybe I got used to it with Robert; I don't know. It doesn't bother me a lot to know I have it. Oh, there are times when I look in the mirror and say to myself, " 'Lady, you've got cancer.' It puts a strange feeling through me for a moment. But it doesn't last for long. I think I'm getting accustomed to it now.

"I suppose it would be different if I'd always had good health," she went on. Raymond's attention was all focused on his aunt now. He watched as she patted the crutches that leaned against her rocker. "I've learned a lot from these."

A few minutes later, they were on their way home. "I've learned a lot from these… I've learned a lot from these… I've learned a lot from these…" The words swirled over and over through Raymond's mind. "Mother, why does Aunt Sally have crutches?" he asked.

"Why, Raymond! Don't you know?" Mother's voice showed her incredulity.

Raymond shook his head. "I don't think I ever thought about them until this evening. She's always had them. They're like a part of her. I don't think I even wondered until now."

Mother nodded slowly. "I suppose that's understandable," she agreed. "Sally's crutches have been with her since long before you were born. It was an accident. Her lower back was injured, and she's never walked since without crutches. It happened when she was just your age—nineteen. I barely remember it, for she's fourteen years older than I am.

"From talks we've had since I grew up, I know it was a major adjustment for her. She says, however, that once she gave up wondering why it had to happen to her and just accepted it as God's will for her life, she found peace and rest. She has led a full life in spite of her handicap, of course, just as you're learning to do yourself. Her dreams of working in a children's home never came to pass, but she was blessed with a family of her own instead."

"Oh, Mother. I don't think you know how often I feel sorry for myself!" Raymond replied. "Aunt Sally puts me to shame. There's still so much I can do!"

"There always will be, Son," Father encouraged. "You know how much you appreciate your aunt, even though she's very limited physically, and will likely become more so as time goes on. It's not what Aunt Sally can do that makes her important to you; it's what she is. No handicap will ever rob her of her personality. Nor do you need to let yours rob you of anything God has for you."

Raymond knew that the things his parents said were true. But still, what could he actually do for the Lord? Had his burden to reach souls on the mission field—a burden he had carried since he was first converted—not come from God after all? Had he just imagined that in the future he might be called by the church to active service at one of the overseas missions?

"Oh, Father," he prayed, "what do You want me to do? Whatever it is, I want to be willing to do it. Aunt Sally wanted to work in a children's home, but that wasn't in Your plan. I want to serve on the mission field, but if that isn't in Your plan either, then help me to accept that too."

A few days later an early morning phone call brought Raymond to the living room. "Brother Raymond," the voice on the other end of the connection said, "this is Nelson Graham from Centertown. I'm sure you know that our school teacher, Sister Miriam, plans to be married this summer. She won't be coming back to the classroom, of course. We are in need of someone to replace her, and several brethren suggested your name.

"As you're aware, this is a mission setting," Brother Nelson went on. "The congregation here was started to provide fellowship for several people who were looking for a more scriptural church than the area had to offer before we came.

"This means that we have a number of children in our classrooms who don't have any or hardly any religious training," he added. "The school is therefore very instrumental in taking the Gospel into those homes through the printed material the children take home, as well as through the principles that are instilled in them in the classroom setting."

Brother Nelson was silent then, but Raymond could think of nothing to say. Teaching was something he had always been sure the Lord would not ask of him. "I'll have to think about it," he managed to say at last. "I'll get back in touch with you in a few days."

During the following days, a mixture of denial and genuine heart searching wrestled with each other in Raymond's thoughts. He desperately wanted God's will for his life—wanted it regardless of what it might be. But he also desperately wanted not to teach school.

The longer he thought about it and prayed about it, however, the more convinced he became that the denial came from his own carnal will. He had never wanted to teach school, and he did not want to now. And yet, might this be as close as he would ever get to an active mission field?

"Oh, Father," he prayed at last, "empty me completely of all my own ideas and ambitions and desires. Put into my heart exactly the aspirations and goals You want to be there instead. I give myself up completely, Lord. I want to live for Your glory and Yours alone. I want Your will in every area of my life—nothing more, nothing less, and nothing else."

Six months later, Raymond stood at the door of his classroom one afternoon watching his students leave for their various homes at the end of another busy and interesting school day. Some of them were on their way to a loving welcome by godly parents who had missed them and were eagerly anticipating their return from school. Others were returning to homes where carnal selfishness led to unhappiness and even to misery. Each of them carried with him some little message from the Word of God—a message that Raymond had purposely designed to appeal to the yearnings of those parents who did not yet know Jesus as their personal Savior.

"Lord, how wondrously You work!" he marveled as he watched them go. "Aunt Sally couldn't fulfill her dream of working in a children's home, and I can't fulfill my dream of serving in a mission overseas. You chose not to let me take the Gospel to the ends of the earth, Father, but You did allow me to take it to these children as they come into my classroom.

"Help me to faithfully give them the message of Your Word, Father. Some of them are already old enough to be accountable to You. Those who come from homes where the Gospel isn't the parents' guide for life are old enough to carry the message of salvation to their parents, even if they aren't old enough to respond to it yet themselves. And meanwhile, the seed is being sown in their hearts as well. You have given me a marvelous opportunity to reach out to needy souls right here on this mission field.

"I was tempted to think I wouldn't be good for anything, and here You've given me more to do for You than an entire lifetime will be long enough to accomplish. Help me to be like Aunt Sally, Lord, faithfully doing the things I can, and not allowing myself to worry about the things that are beyond me because of my handicap. Help me to serve You faithfully on my mission field at home!"

Brown Leaf

A lone, shriveled leaf at the top of a tree
Flutters in wind and snow.
Little brown leaf at the top of the tree,
Why don't you just let go?

Why don't you flutter down to the ground
And hide in the winter snow?
There the winds don't beat and the storms don't rage.
Why don't you just let go?

Soft on the bosom of Mother Earth,
Quiet and sweet and slow,
Gently into the welcoming night,
Why don't you just let go?

"I didn't place me here," said the leaf.
"I didn't choose to grow;
"But there's One Who did, and 'tis He alone
"Will choose when I shall let go.

"Until that day, I've a purpose here,
"Not all of which I know;
"But I'll smile at the storm and I'll sing in the gale
"Till the Master lets me go!"

The Living Proof

"THAT HOUSE TRAILER WASN'T here three weeks ago!" Kenneth Gray exclaimed. He braked the family car to a stop at the end of the driveway to their new property. Directly across the road from them, a house trailer was parked in the open field—a trailer that had not been there when they bought their new place three weeks earlier.

"It certainly wasn't," Diane agreed. "I wonder who our neighbors will be and what they'll be like. We sure hadn't expected anyone this close!"

Kenneth shrugged. "So much for the privacy we thought we'd have," he said. "Oh well, the Lord knew before we bought this property that by the time we moved here we'd have neighbors."

"The idea will take a while to get used to," Diane said.

"We hadn't expected anyone on our doorstep."

"Or almost on it anyhow," Kenneth agreed. "Now I'm doubly glad we have a long driveway! I wonder whether these people have children?"

"It could make complications for us if they do," Diane answered. "We liked the privacy here because we felt it would give us better control of our children's environment than a setting with close neighbors would."

"Well, they're here now," Kenneth said. "We'll have to take things one day at a time, looking to the Lord to meet our needs."

Getting settled into their new home kept the Grays' minds occupied for several days, and they almost forgot the house trailer across the road. There was no one there, nor was any work in progress to get electricity and water and sewage in place.

Then one morning several service vehicles arrived almost at the same time, and feverish activity began. The well driller pounded away on one side of the yard, while a backhoe dug trenches for a septic tank and tile bed behind the trailer. Meanwhile, the electricians were busy getting the power connected.

Two days later, the installations were finished. The following morning, a car, a moving truck, and two loaded pickups arrived.

"I'm going over to see if they need help," Kenneth told Diane. "Though with all the vehicles there, I suspect they have as much assistance as they can use."

A few minutes later he was home again. "They have more help now than they can put to work efficiently," he said. "We'll wait to go over until they've had time to get organized. By the way, they have two boys, just the sizes of ours."

Several times in the weeks that followed the Grays walked over to call on their new neighbors, but no one was ever at home. Two vehicles had stayed when the movers left, but now they almost always seemed to be gone. By the time they both got home in the evening, it was too late for the Grays to feel comfortable to go calling.

"We'll surely catch them sometime," Diane said as they walked home after their third frustrated effort. "Maybe we'll have to call ahead and arrange a time that suits them."

"I've thought about that," Kenneth agreed. "I could call late enough some evening that they would be sure to be home."

The following Thursday, the Grays again walked to their neighbors after supper. This time, both vehicles were in the yard, and the Feltons' two sons met them at the end of their drive.

While the Grays were glad for an opportunity to meet the Feltons, they soon learned that they and their neighbors had very little in common. Dan offered Kenneth a bottle of beer before he had shown him a chair, and a cloud of cigarette smoke constantly swirled about the room. Rock music from the stereo that no one offered to turn down made it almost impossible to visit. Before long, the Grays gathered their family together and walked back home, leaving the Feltons with an invitation to visit them sometime.

Week after week all they saw or heard from the other side of the road was the occasional arrival or departure of a vehicle. Then one evening while Kenneth was cultivating in the field next to the house, a pickup arrived in their yard. Dan Felton, their neighbor, got out and waited for Kenneth and the tractor to return to the side of the field where he was.

"Good evening," Kenneth greeted his guest as he turned off the tractor.

"Evening," Dan returned briefly. He pointed toward the land that Kenneth had just finished working. "There's one thing obvious anyhow," he said. "You don't know how to farm!"

"I see." Kenneth was not sure how to reply. "I guess I'm just doing the best I know. Maybe it's not a good way."

"Not in this country, it isn't!" Dan answered. "Around here you never plow more than three or four inches deep. You're digging into that ground a good nine inches. Would you happen to have a sledgehammer I could borrow?" he went on in the same breath. "I need to drive a few stakes over there, and I never did own a sledgehammer. Thought maybe you'd have one you aren't using at the moment."

"Sure," Kenneth agreed. He swung down from the tractor seat. "It's in the shed over there." He pointed toward a small building between the house and the barn. "I'll be happy to let you use it. Do you need a hand with the job?"

Kenneth was glad for the opportunity to assist his neighbor. The necessary stakes were soon in place, and once again, in spite of his earlier explanation that he never used alcohol, Dan Felton offered him a bottle of beer.

Later that evening, Kenneth told Diane about Dan's analysis of his farming skills. He was almost laughing as he concluded, "The most amusing part was that he obviously doesn't know much about farming himself. He was criticizing me for plowing nine inches deep, saying that in this area you don't dare to plow more than three or four inches deep. I was going nine inches deep all right, but I wasn't plowing; I was cultivating. I wasn't turning the soil at all, just stirring it around!"

During the winter months that followed, the Grays saw very little of their neighbors. Occasionally one of them would come to borrow something. And often when the Grays next needed that item, someone had to go across the road to collect it. Very few of the items the Feltons borrowed found their own way home. It was not that they intended to keep them; they just never got around to bringing them back.

One evening late in the following June, Kenneth and

Diane and their children were working in the garden. Dan Felton drove into their yard and came to where Kenneth was working. "Don't know what you ever did to that patch of ground," he stated, pointing across the lane to the field where Kenneth had been cultivating during Dan's call the previous fall. "I've never seen grain grow like that in this country before! Can I borrow your skill saw?" he added in the same breath.

Later that evening, Kenneth and Diane discussed their relationship with their neighbors. "You hardly get a word in edgewise," Kenneth said. "And that's on any subject, let alone a word for the Lord. Dan never stops talking, or almost never. I wonder when he thinks!"

"Well, we can pray for them, whether they let us talk to them or not," Diane said. "They certainly need to find the Lord as their Savior!"

Months went by, with the relationship between the two families continuing the same. Then one day about three years after they had moved, Kenneth came home with some exciting news.

"The Feltons are going to church at the chapel up the road," he said. "From what I heard, they both became Christians recently."

"The Feltons became Christians!" Diane's voice showed her amazement. "Are you sure?"

Kenneth nodded. "Pete Jackson told me, and I've no reason to question his word." He hesitated a moment, then went on, "Are you surprised that our prayers are being answered? Well, don't feel alone. I must admit that I wasn't prepared for this. It makes me eager to visit them again."

"Me too. When do you think it would suit?"

A few days later the Grays were seated in the Feltons' living room. This time no beer was offered, and the cigarette smoke and rock music of the previous visit were missing.

A few pleasantries were exchanged, then Kenneth said, "I heard some good news the other day. Someone told me you folks found the Lord Jesus as your Savior."

Dan smiled a little as he answered. "News does have a way of getting around, doesn't it? Yes, it's true. We just found out what we've been missing all these years. I guess we could say that no one ever told us before, but that wouldn't really be fair; up until now, we wouldn't have wanted to listen."

"So what piqued your interest now?" Kenneth asked. "Something must have changed."

"It did," Dan agreed. "I'll be more than happy to tell you what it was." He hesitated a moment, then went on slowly. "You knew my business wasn't going well? And that Daisy here was about to pack up her things and the boys and leave me here alone?"

Kenneth shook his head. "Maybe we're too busy with our own affairs to be as concerned as we should be about others' needs. We hadn't known."

"It all traces back to the drink," Dan admitted. "I'm

almost bankrupt along with all my other problems. One day a while ago, I was sitting here feeling sorry for myself because everything was against me. I was drinking, of course. Well, someone knocked on the door, and in came Gene Watson. Now you probably don't know Gene. He's a tough character, a lot like I was. A year or so ago Gene got religion, as they say around here. I don't see him much, so I really hadn't gotten to know him as a Christian.

"Well, Gene sat on that chair," Dan went on, "and he never said a word for a long time. Then finally he told me point-blank, 'Dan, you've got enough trouble for a dozen men. There's only one way to get yourself out of this; give the whole mess to God and let Him take over. If you really give yourself up to Him, He'll figure out the details. It's working for me, and it will work for you as well.'

"For about the first three seconds, I was boiling mad. I had almost told him to leave real quick, when I got to thinking. Do you know what I did then? I told him how things really were instead. I said, 'Gene, two or three years ago, if you'd have said that to me, I'd have told you real fast to get out of here and not come back. But the living proof that what you're saying is true has been walking around right across the road from me for three years now. You're right. I need to give my life to God. It's working for the Grays, and I can't see why it wouldn't help me too.'"

Kenneth and Diane looked at each other, but neither

of them spoke. Finally Kenneth said, "I see. Well, give the Lord the credit, Dan. It's only by His grace that we can live the way we do. And we make mistakes sometimes, you know. It's just that you don't see them."

Dan nodded. "I'm not expecting anyone to be perfect," he said. "But you people have proved to me that it's possible to come a whole lot closer than I was coming!"

"We went and talked to the preacher yet that evening," Daisy added. "Dan found the Lord then. It took me a while, but a few days later, after I'd seen the dramatic change in him, I knew that what he had was the answer for me too. So we went back to the preacher again, and that time I finally understood what it meant to repent and to trust in the shed blood of Jesus for forgiveness. And my, what a difference it's making in our lives!"

"We can see at least some aspects of those changes, just being here in your home this evening," Kenneth said.

Daisy grinned. "No more beer. No more smoking. No more cursing. No more wondering when Dan will ever get home—and whether, when he does, he'll find some reason to beat up on me or the boys."

"No more rock music either," Dan added with a grin in his wife's direction. "I see now that I was using it for an excuse, but it's a fact that Daisy's music made it hard for me to enjoy being here."

"No more rock music," Daisy agreed with a blush. "That was my real weakness. I loved rock music. But the first time I turned it on after I gave my heart to the Lord, I couldn't stand the sound of it anymore. Just like that, the appetite was gone."

They visited a while longer, with Kenneth and Diane both encouraging the Feltons to find a church where the members were living according to the teachings of the New Testament. Kenneth also invited them to come to church with them sometime. Then the Grays went home.

"They surely gave us some things to think about," Kenneth said as they walked back to their own house. "We thought our attempts to witness to them of the things of the Lord were in vain. And all the while they were watching our lives and seeing Christ within us. How could we have thought they had no interest in spiritual things?"

"It makes me marvel," Diane agreed. "It's humbling too. I wonder how much they saw in me that made it harder for them to make the choice they did. They sure could have picked out failures had they looked for them."

"In me too," Kenneth added. "I wonder if the Lord didn't blind them to our faults so that all they took notice of were the things that drew them to Him."

"And let them overlook the things that could have been stumbling blocks," Diane added. "It makes me wonder whether other people might be watching us too."

"In some areas, the chapel up the road isn't teaching

the entire Gospel," Kenneth said slowly. "While we have growing to do too, both as individuals and as a congregation, I am convinced that we want to do what we can to encourage the Feltons to attend a more scriptural church."

"It will be a challenge for all of us," Diane added. "Are we letting our lights shine as brightly as the Lord of the church desires? Or is there more we could be doing to draw other souls to Him?"

Kenneth nodded. "The Feltons sure didn't appeal to me as very likely candidates for salvation. Let's take it as a lesson that there's no one too hopeless for the Lord. We also need to understand that there's no true Christian that the Lord can't use as living proof, as Dan calls us, that Christianity works."

Deliverance

There's never a heart so wayward
But Jesus can forgive;
There's never a soul so sinful
But can look to Him and live.

For the blood of Christ, the Savior,
That was spilled on Calvary
Can atone for all vile actions
And can set your spirit free.

It can give you supreme deliverance;
It can calm and soothe your fears;
It can make you a transformed person
For all your remaining years.

And though nature may ne'er forgive you—
Though your past scars remain—
Yet the sin sores cleansed at Calvary
Need never hurt again.

Jessica or Lima Beans?

ESTHER JEAN STARED AT the rows of lima beans. The garden had matured slowly this year, and she had not yet picked any limas. But now, early in September, the pods were hanging thick and almost full. Would she get them picked before frost? Maybe she should pick some of them this evening, even though they weren't quite ready.

"But you've been thinking about Jessica all day," her conscience reminded her. "She's old and lonely, you know. And you've put off going to see her several times during the past few weeks, even when you felt strongly that you should go. Now all day you've been feeling that the Lord especially wants you to visit her yet this evening. And David agreed before he left for his school board meeting that you should do it now."

"But what if there's frost? I know we have an abundance of other vegetables, but I was so much hoping for limas yet too."

"Jessica doesn't have anyone who really cares for her," the little voice suggested. "She's old and almost always alone in her house there beside the river. How can you help her to find Me if you ignore her? And don't forget that David thought you should go yet this evening."

"But the lima beans, Lord! I didn't think to mention them to David. If I had, he might have suggested that I pick them this evening and visit Jessica some other time."

Esther Jean moved slowly toward the shed. She'd get a bucket and pick a few of the limas, she thought. That way, if there was frost, they'd have gotten some of them. Maybe later this evening she could visit Jessica.

Soon Esther Jean was snapping off handfuls of pods and dropping them into her pail. In what seemed like a very little while, the pail was full. "Daniel," she called to their oldest son, "please bring another bucket for me. I want to pick more of these lima beans."

Soon the second pail was full, and Esther Jean asked Daniel to bring a basket from the shed. She dumped both buckets of beans into the hamper and continued to pick the almost-ready beans.

"What about Jessica?" the Holy Spirit prompted as she dropped the last few pods into the third bucketful. "It's getting late. If you don't go soon, she'll be in bed."

Esther Jean sighed. The lima picking was going so well, and she could almost feel a nip of frost in the air. The beans would certainly be ruined if she left them on the plants. Surely if she had thought to mention them to David, he would have told her to pick them instead of going to see Jessica.

"Tomorrow, Lord," she decided. "Tomorrow I'll visit Jessica." And she went on picking the almost-ready beans.

When David and Esther Jean got up the next morning, she hurried to check the temperature. Had there been frost? As she stepped outside to read the thermometer, she felt raindrops on her face.

"There wasn't any frost after all," she told David when she came in. "The limas could have been left to get more mature."

"The limas?" David raised his eyebrows. "They were hardly ready yet. Surely you didn't pick them all last evening? I thought you were going to visit Jessica."

Esther Jean shook her head. "I was planning to," she said slowly. "But then I thought about the limas. And it felt so cold that I was about sure there would be frost by this morning. So I worked on them instead."

David sighed when she had finished speaking. "I thought about the limas too," he said. "But I could tell by the pain in my leg that was broken that it was going to rain. That's why I suggested you visit Jessica instead of picking them."

David went to the barn then, and Esther Jean went about her morning work. She was mixing pancakes for breakfast when the phone rang.

"Hello. It's Weavers," she said into the receiver.

"Esther Jean, this is Rose Jackson," the voice on the other end said. "Did you hear about Jessica Payne?"

"Jessica?" Esther Jean felt herself go weak. "No. What happened?" She had a feeling that she didn't want to know.

"Jessica drowned in the river last night," Rose answered. "First thing this morning, Jason Stewart went down to the dock at his cottage, and there was her body, partly in and partly out of the water near the shore. No one knows what happened, but I thought that since you knew her well, you'd want to know."

"Thanks for calling." It was all Esther Jean could say. She sat down quickly, feeling as though she might faint.

Later that afternoon, they heard the remainder of the story. When the police went into Jessica's house, they found a note on the table.

"No one cares about me," it read. "Hardly ever does anyone come to see me. If no one comes to visit me yet this evening, I'm going to jump into the river at eleven o'clock."

The Problem with Eric

"I'M SORRY, ERIC, BUT you'll have to do this again." Sister Helen struggled to hold back the frustration in her voice as she returned his soiled and rumpled paper to an equally soiled and rumpled boy. "Not only is your paper messy," she added, "but most of the answers are wrong."

Sullen but silent, the second grader trudged back to his desk. Sister Helen knew he would be stomping his feet if he thought he could get by with it. She sighed. At the beginning of the term, he had done just that. He had quickly learned not to, of course. But some of his other unlovable habits were not so easily unlearned.

"I don't know whether I'll be able to cope with him for a whole school year or not," Helen confided to her mother that evening. "I think I expend more energy on Eric than on all the other students together."

Mother nodded. "Teaching him is a big job, isn't it?" Her sympathetic tone told Helen she understood, and Mother's sympathy encouraged her to share further.

Helen knew that Mother's understanding was born of close contact with Eric's family. Mother had made it her business to spend time with Eric's mother each week ever since the family had started attending the church where Father served as a minister. But Helen did not realize that there was a chapter of the story she was not aware of.

Everyone in the congregation had rejoiced when Eric's father and mother found the Lord as their Savior and Friend. And everyone was glad that they wanted their only child to attend a Christian day school.

Helen sighed heavily now as she remembered how happy she had been about their decision. "I'm so glad," she had told her friend Lucy. "Christian schooling is very important."

But that had been before the chairman of the school board had knocked on Helen's front door one April evening with an invitation to teach the following year.

"I actually thought even then that I'd be able to handle him," she admitted to Mother now. "I didn't realize what it would be like to keep tabs on him and his antics for more than thirty hours every week. He must use at least half of his time thinking up pranks, and he spends most of the other half trying them. With his careless work and his couldn't-care-less attitude, Eric is becoming more than I can cope with."

Mother nodded again, and when Helen did not continue, she said, "I'm not with Eric's mother for thirty hours each week. I suspect, however, that I'd need an abundant portion of the grace of God if I were. The carelessness and lack of order in their home really tries me. It's not as bad as it used to be, though."

Mother's voice trailed off, and Helen wondered which was not as bad anymore, the lack of order or the degree to which the disorder bothered her mother.

"I realized from the start that neither parent had any religious training," Mother went on. "But it's more than the absence of religious influence. That home lacks order more than many ungodly homes do. They're trying to do better now, but learning will take time and practice."

"And much patience on our part," Helen added. "I'm afraid my patience will run out before they've had enough practice to make it work."

"It will," Mother agreed. "Mine did."

"Yours!" Helen dropped the dress she was hemming. "What do you mean, yours did?" Never had she known Mother to run out of patience.

"I mean just what I said," Mother replied. "I hadn't realized it myself, but Father brought it to my attention. I was expecting too much too soon. I could understand that easily enough when Father and I talked about it. But it was harder to understand that their unlovable ways were not really the root of my problem with loving them.

"Father helped me to see that I lacked genuine long-suffering love—the love of God reaching out through me to them. He said I wasn't seeing them as Jesus saw them." Mother shook her head now, and her expression was sad. "It was hard, but at last I realized that he was right. The root of my problem was me, not them.

"It's still true that there are some real needs in their home," Mother continued. "But once I accepted the fact that there wasn't enough love in me to meet those needs, I asked the Lord to use me as a channel for His love, so that it could flow through me to them. Without that, all I could do was fail, and fail again."

Mother hesitated. When Helen did not speak, she continued. "You'll find it the same in working with Eric," she said. "There's only one key to his heart, the love of God. Eric needs that love desperately, and you're there to give it.

"But you can't do it of yourself. It isn't possible. You're a sincere Christian, and you want to do the very best for each of your students. So far, you haven't been able to reach Eric, though. I think it's because you still haven't found how to give him the kind of love he needs—to love him as though he were your own little brother. You can't do that on your own; it has to be the love of Jesus working through you. Once that happens, Eric won't need his defenses anymore."

"Thanks, Mother," Helen said slowly. "I'll need some time to think this over." She rose to go to her room.

"Mother is likely right," she mused as she went. "Eric's

problem is rooted in his need to be accepted and loved. Loved with a careful and caring love that will give him security. Then his need for extra attention will melt away, and he will be free to be a contented and happy child."

Helen knew, as Mother had told her, that the ability to give the kind of love Eric needed was not in her, though. "Lord, make me a channel of Your love," she prayed then. "Use me in whatever way is necessary to release Eric from his defenses and set him free to be a normal boy. Father, I want to love him the way You do— or at least the way I love Roger and James, who are my brothers."

As her mother had warned her, it was not always easy. Eric still needed discipline and careful watching. But he did learn to do his work well, mostly because he learned to love his teacher and wanted to please her.

And when Helen's family moved to a different community, she found that she missed Eric more than any of her other students.

Should I Confess?

A SERIOUS-FACED YOUNG MOTHER knelt by her bed in the early dawn. "Search my heart, Father," she prayed. "Help me to do as Brother Benjamin advised us all in his sermon last evening. Give me eyes that see my own failures, Lord, and courage to do what needs to be done to correct them. Show me myself as You see me, and give me the wisdom I need to serve You faithfully. If there's anything in my life that displeases You, please help me to recognize it and to do whatever is needful to make it right."

Dora's prayer went on, covering many areas of concern to a young mother who was endeavoring to serve her Lord well in all of life. A few minutes later she was in the kitchen preparing breakfast for her family.

Quickly she filled two lunch boxes. "Why don't I put

a chocolate cream in each of them?" she asked herself. "It's been a good while since the children had candy in their lunches."

Standing on tiptoe, she opened the cupboard above her head. Candy was a rare treat in their household, and when there was any it was stored well out of reach.

She pulled the white bag down from the shelf and reaching in removed two lumps of chocolate. She had just dropped one into the first lunch box when her hand stopped in midair and she gasped.

"Why, I forgot about that years ago already!" she exclaimed aloud, perplexed at the sudden remembrance of a little girl and a piece of chocolate candy.

With amazing clarity, her memory replayed the incident of twenty-six years before. She and her brother George had been attending a small country school at the time. The local general store was located nearby, and when their mother needed just a few items from the store, she would send a note to the teacher, asking her to excuse George from the school grounds at lunchtime so he could get the needed supplies.

One lovely morning in September when Dora was in third grade, she had been allowed to accompany George on his trip to the store. She could still remember how she had run to keep pace with his long strides.

Once they were inside the cluttered building, George had gone about his errands, leaving her to occupy herself as she wished, giving only the big-brotherly admonition not to break anything. As Dora examined first one item and then another with her eyes (she knew better than to touch them), the storekeeper went with her brother to the back of the room to measure the lamp wick Mother needed.

While they were gone, Dora happened to walk past the boxes of candy on display along the front of the long wooden counter. Chocolate creams were her favorite, and here was a whole carton of them! She checked to be sure that both George and the storekeeper were still out of sight, and that no one else was coming from outside.

No one would see! She slipped a lump of the candy into her mouth. The flavor was delightful at first, but before she was half finished chewing it, her conscience began to torment her and she hardly noticed the coveted taste anymore.

Glancing over her shoulder, she hurried outside where she waited until George was ready to return to school. She never begged to go along to the store again. In the years between, she had completely forgotten about that chocolate cream candy.

Dora snapped the fasteners shut on her children's lunch boxes. The tramp of feet on the back porch was announcing the arrival of the chore crew.

With an effort, she dismissed the scene in the store from her mind and went about her usual morning duties. Soon the older children were off to school, and the younger ones were playing church in the living room.

The day was a busy one, and the thought of chocolate candy disappeared until the older boys deposited their lunch boxes on the counter when they came home from school. That brought back the unwelcome scene again.

"Whatever shall I do about it?" she wondered in dismay. "One candy is such a little thing. Does a grown woman go to someone to confess that twenty-six years ago she stole a piece of candy? I'm sure he'd think I was being ridiculous!"

But the memory of the little girl with the chocolate was not to be dismissed. As Dora prepared supper and cared for the little ones, she struggled with the memory of that candy.

Soon the tramp of snowy feet again announced the arrival of the chore crew, and Dora hurried to get the food onto the table and the baby into her high chair.

The children chattered as usual during the meal, but their mother scarcely heard what they were saying. Two hours later, the day's work was finished and the children were in bed. When they were all settled for the night, Don and Dora sat in the kitchen, drinking tea. They always enjoyed these times together when the children were in bed.

Dora thought of the chocolate candy again. But what was the right thing to do about it? she wondered. It was the only item she had ever stolen, and it was so very long ago. She had been but a child at the time. Was she accountable now for her action then?

Don's voice brought her attention back to the present. "What's on your mind, Dear?" he repeated when she admitted that she had not heard what he had said. "You're not your usual happy self."

As his blue eyes met her brown ones, she could plainly read his concern. "So it shows, does it?" she said slowly.

Don nodded, but made no further comment, and Dora knew he was waiting for her to explain.

Soon the whole story was out, and Dora was wiping her tears. "I hardly know what to do," she concluded. "Does the Lord expect me to confess such a little thing as a piece of candy, especially after twenty-six years?"

Don looked thoughtful. "What do you think?" he probed.

Dora hesitated. She had hoped he would make that decision for her. Yet deep down she knew she ought to make it herself. She nodded slowly. "I guess I don't know of any reason why He wouldn't," she admitted. "But why did I have to think of it after all this time? Why didn't He remind me sooner if He wanted me to confess it?"

"I don't know," Don answered soberly. "But now that He has reminded you, we know what needs to be done, don't we?"

She nodded again. "Can we plan to go to town tomorrow, then? Wilson's store moved to Rockford twenty years ago. I'd like to get it looked after right away."

At quarter past ten the following morning, Dora left Wilson's store. There were tears in her eyes, but her heart was singing. Soon she was at home again, going about her work with her usual enjoyment. The oppressed feeling she had labored under the day before seemed almost like a dream. She thought about the candy only once, and then it was just to wonder why it had been so long before God had brought it to her attention.

That evening as she knelt to pray before going to bed, she thanked the Lord for the experience. "If there's anything else in my life that doesn't please You, Lord, help me to take care of it too."

The thought trailed off as Dora recognized the answer to her question of the evening before, when she had asked why God took so long to bring the candy to her mind. "You revealed this to me after all these years because I asked You to, didn't You, Lord?" she prayed then. "Yesterday morning I asked You to show me anything in my life that displeases You.

"Thank you for Your answer. And thank you for giving me the courage to make it right with Mr. Wilson. Also, if there's anything else I need to make right, please bring it to my mind."

The next morning Dora slipped a chocolate candy into each lunch box again. This time when she did so, her heart rejoiced.

All Such Desires

"WHEN COURTING COUPLES HOLD hands, it's a sure manifestation that the flesh isn't crucified as it ought to be. If you don't agree with me that the desire for physical contact with someone who is not yet your husband or wife comes from the flesh, then tell me where it does come from!" Brother John went on speaking on courtship standards for Christians, but Roy's thoughts were no longer on the message.

Over and over his mind repeated the evangelist's challenge: "If it doesn't come from the flesh, where does it come from? If it doesn't come from the flesh, where does it come from? If it doesn't come from the flesh, where does it come from?"

Mentally Roy shook himself. "Come, come," he thought, "you've not heard another thing he's said. Listen to the sermon now. You can think about holding hands once you're back in your room."

But the faithful voice of the Spirit of God was not to be readily silenced. "If it doesn't come from the flesh, where does it come from?" Roy dropped his head and closed his eyes as the turmoil within continued. He surveyed his and Nancy's courtship candidly. A number of couples in their congregation held hands occasionally, some of them more than others. Unfortunately, very little teaching had been given against the practice. He and Nancy held hands once in a while too, not having given much thought to the possibility that it might not be a good idea.

Now here he was listening to a godly man he had come to respect highly—a man who insisted that when courting couples held hands, they were giving in to the desires of the flesh. Such conduct displeased the Lord, Brother John insisted, and must be confessed and forsaken if one were to live in victory.

Suddenly the minister's words caught his attention again. "All the desires I've been talking about come from the sinful nature," he said. "But that doesn't mean you can't do anything to control them. God is more than able to help you to crucify these fleshly desires. He wants to place within you the urge to do His will instead. But you must see your failure as sin first, and repent of it as such. Only then can the Lord work in your life to give you victory.

"It isn't necessary for anyone to live in bondage to these fleshly desires," the evangelist went on. "God is just as able to give you victory over wrong thoughts and actions of the nature I've been talking about as He is to give the drunkard victory over drink or the smoker over tobacco. You might still be tempted at times, but if the flesh is truly crucified, you'll no longer allow yourself to entertain any desire for the practices that you've repented of. As soon as the temptation comes, you'll call on the Lord and ask for a way of escape."

Soon the sermon ended, and Roy went back to his room. Dinner hour came, but Roy remained sitting on the side of his bed in the deserted room. "I still don't see how such a little thing as holding hands occasionally can be so wrong!" he reasoned.

"But after what Brother John said this morning, how can you still think it's right?" the Spirit contended quietly. "Why not admit you've been wrong, and forsake this practice just as you would any other sin that was brought to your attention?"

Still silent, Roy sat thinking a few minutes longer. At last he slid on his knees beside the bed. "You know all about this, Father," he prayed silently. "I really do want Your will in all of my life. Now You've brought this practice to my attention. Brother John called it sin, Lord. I hadn't thought of it that way before. Yet I'm sure Brother John was serious. He must have a reason to call it sin. Help me to see it as You want me to, Lord."

Roy waited in silence on his knees, allowing God to search his heart, and gradually his thinking began to change. Why had he not questioned the practice before? Why had he and Nancy begun it anyway? What was its purpose?

"I think I'm beginning to see the evangelist's point, Father," he prayed. "Thank you for bringing it to my attention. Brother John's reasoning has to be right, of course; when courting couples hold hands, there is no purpose aside from the gratification of the flesh. I don't want to leave any room in my life for that. I accept that when courting couples hold hands it is sin. I'm sorry not to have recognized it as such before.

"I need Your power to crucify the old nature that still wants to experience this unlawful enjoyment, Father. And I need You to reveal any other areas in my life that aren't pleasing to You. Give me grace and courage to make the adjustments You want."

As Roy rose from his knees a few minutes later, the turmoil and unrest within had vanished. The Lord was faithfully fulfilling His promise that those who confess and forsake their sins shall find mercy. The troubling voice of the Spirit had ceased, and instead of conviction for wrongdoing He was bringing assurance of sins forgiven and the promise of victory over further temptation.

"Thank you, Father," Roy whispered as he removed his writing paper from the dresser drawer. Determinedly he set about the task before him. He began:

Dear Nancy,

Greetings in the precious Name of Jesus. This will be a brief note, for it's soon time to leave for cottage meeting.

Brother John preached about courtship standards this morning. He said that holding hands and other practices that bring physical contact between a dating couple are wrong—that it's the work of the flesh, designed to fulfill the lusts thereof. I didn't agree with him at first, but as long as I tried to defend what we've been doing, I didn't have peace. As soon as I admitted that it's just like he said, and confessed it to the Lord as sin, I had peace and rest again.

I wanted to tell you about this right away. I think you will understand. If you don't, please pray about it humbly and submissively, asking the Lord to show you as He did me. I know you want to please Him well in all things. May He bless you abundantly.

Roy finished the letter and got it ready to send. As he dropped it into the outgoing mail, a new thought entered his mind. What if Nancy failed to see it as he did now? What if she still thought they should go on as they had before? What would he do then?

"Lord, You know all about this," he prayed. "You know that Nancy might not understand. Help her to, Father. You know I care about her, and want her to please You. You know, too, that if she doesn't agree with Brother John's scriptural conclusion, then it will be necessary for us to stop dating. I don't want that, Lord; I want to keep on seeing her. But I want Your will even more than I want Nancy. Help me to rest in You now, confident that whatever her response may be, it will be Your will for me, even if it isn't Your will for her."

It was time to leave for cottage meeting. "I think I know what her answer will be," Roy concluded as he slid into his suit coat. "But if I'm wrong, I'll know this is the Lord's way of telling me that Nancy isn't the girl He has for me."

Twenty-seven Years

SIXTY-TWO-YEAR-OLD RONALD JAVIN ADJUSTED the paper on his clipboard and cleaned his glasses. People were settling in all around him as the time for the afternoon session of the Bible Conference neared.

"Restitution is a new twist for me," he commented to the man who was sitting to his left. "I've been a Christian for only six months, though. Maybe it's all old information for you?"

The other man nodded. "In a way, I suppose you could say it is. I've known the Lord as my Savior for forty-nine years. I keep on learning, though. At meetings like this, you never know what you'll hear. The speakers' ideas have astounded me sometimes. Yet when I look them up in the Bible, there they are. I just hadn't seen them before."

A hush fell over the audience as a gray-haired man

in a dark suit moved to the front of the auditorium. "We have two topics this afternoon," he said. "The first deals with restitution, and will be given by Brother Daniel."

The speaker who had been announced walked briskly to the front, where a blackboard had been placed for his use. Picking up the chalk, he said, "We plan to be very practical today, folks."

As he spoke, he wrote Bill S. in large letters on the blackboard. "All right. Bill here represents somebody in your past. You might not have known Bill well, but you and he were acquainted. For some reason, Bill managed to bother you. And because he was in your way, or you thought he was, you did him wrong…"

The speaker's voice went on, but Ronald Javin did not hear what he said. Ronald had not heard much of what the speaker had said ever since he wrote the name on the blackboard: Bill S.

Ronald stared at the letters again, and he felt as though his head had begun to spin—a spin that accelerated by the second. A spin that soon, he thought, would make him dizzy.

Bill S. He looked at the letters again. Yes, that was what they said. Exactly. He shook his head, trying to clear the dizziness that threatened to overpower him.

What could this speaker know about him and Bill S.? Ronald began to count. It was twenty-seven years since he had wronged Bill. Bill lived in their community then, and had won a large amount of money from a lottery ticket. Ronald could still taste the bitterness and jealousy that had welled up in his throat when he heard about his neighbor's gambling success.

Bill S. had lived on welfare for as long as Ronald had known him. He had, as he was fond of saying, never done a lick of work in his life and never planned to. Welfare was a great way to live.

Ronald had grown up in a poor home too, but his family had learned to work hard, and had managed to maintain self-respect even though they had very little material goods.

Bill S. used part of his lottery winnings to build the biggest and fanciest house in the area. As soon as he and his wife moved into it, Bill had begun to make degrading comments about the other houses in the community.

Perhaps Ronald Javin came in for more than a fair share of Bill's ribbing, partly because he lived next door and partly because his house was among the smallest in the area. The fact that it was always clean and kept in good repair seemed not to impress the newly rich Bill S.

A few months after Bill and his wife moved in, they went to Florida to escape the northern winter. Bill entertained himself by sending postcards of the balmy South back to his neighbors who were working their way through a severe winter.

One of those postcards set Ronald to thinking about how unfair the situation was. The more he thought about it, the more it bothered him. After all, he could as easily have won the lottery himself. Then he and his wife could have lounged on the Florida beaches while Bill and Jenny shivered here in the North.

The more Ronald thought about it that evening, the more he drank to help himself forget about the unfairness. When he had taken more alcohol than he was used to, he set out for Bill's property. Before the light of another day had brightened the eastern sky, Bill's new house had become a pile of ashes.

Ronald still had the good sense to hide himself at home in bed as soon as the match he struck under the pile of crumpled newspapers on the back porch had produced a sizable blaze. And in the morning, he expressed amazement equal to that of anyone else when he heard that Bill's new house had gone up in flames.

The police didn't question Ronald more than to ask whether he had noticed any unusual activity in the area recently. Everyone assumed that the fire had started by mice eating through the electrical wiring, which is what had happened to another house in the community two years earlier.

But now what? "Restitution applies in every case where you have wronged someone," a voice said then, and Ronald suddenly realized he was sitting in a group of people and was supposed to be listening to a man who was telling them what the Bible says about restitution. Pulling himself together, he tried to concentrate on the speaker's words.

"It doesn't matter who you wronged, and it doesn't matter whether he had it coming. It also doesn't matter how large or small the offense was, and whether anybody ever found out," the speaker went on. "Nor does it matter how long ago it happened. Time doesn't change the need for restitution. Twenty-seven years can go by, but unless you've done something about it, nothing alters. You're just as responsible as the day you did the deed. The passing of a million years could not erase sin!"

Twenty-seven years! Ronald could almost feel the hair stand up on the top of his head. "Twenty-seven years. What made him use that number? Does he know what I did, and he's rubbing it in? But how could he? I've never seen him, and he's never seen me. No one but God and I know who burned Bill's house!"

When Ronald finally forced himself to go to bed that night, he couldn't sleep. "Bill S. Twenty-seven years. Bill S. Twenty-seven years. Bill S. Twenty-seven years." The name and number kept swirling in his brain. At last he got up and sat at the kitchen table, his head propped in his hands. It must have been the Spirit of God who had given the speaker those facts. There simply couldn't be any other source. "Bill S. Twenty-seven years."

The next morning, Ronald Javin drove to town. He stopped in front of the sheriff's office and slowly got out of his car.

"Lord, I still don't have the strength to do this," he prayed. "Since I stopped drinking twenty-some years ago,

I've become a respected citizen in this community. I've not been known to break the law in all that time. Now I'm about to acknowledge that for twenty-seven years I've known I was guilty of a major crime, and I've kept it hidden. What will everyone think of me when they find out?

"You'll have to give me both the words I need and the courage to say them, Lord. Otherwise, this simply won't get done. Of course I realize I have to do it. Restitution must be made. And it has to begin by my owning up to what I did. I don't know what will come of this, Lord. Maybe they'll put me in jail. They could, I suppose. The insurance company paid Bill for his loss. Now they have the right to hold me responsible to repay them. And, anyhow, arson is a criminal offense.

"I burned a man's house for spite and jealousy, Lord. I deserve whatever the law decides to do. I'm going to walk into this sheriff's office now, and by Your grace and in Your strength I'm going to tell the man behind the desk that twenty-seven years ago I burned Bill Strickland's house."

Ronald opened the door and admitted himself inside.

Walking on Coals

THE LAST MILKER PAIL crashed onto its hook above the milk house sink. "There!" Jennifer thought with a grimace. "That hateful job is done for another morning!" She jerked a towel from the roll at her side and dried her dripping hands.

The roar of the milk truck motor interrupted her surging thoughts. She frowned at the clock. Could it be eight-thirty already? Sure enough, it was. "And Mother will have four hours of work for me before it's time to start lunch!" she fumed to herself.

Her thoughts went to the unfinished book she had hoped to read this morning. Or at least she had hoped to before Mother decided this was the morning to houseclean the living room.

The truck driver stepped into the milk house just as

Jennifer's paper towel struck the garbage can. "Morning, Miss Martin," he greeted her in his usual pleasant manner. "It looks as though you don't like towels this morning?" It was partly a question and partly a statement.

Jennifer looked up at him briefly and then back to the crushed wad of paper. "Towels aren't the problem," she retorted. "I don't enjoy having to work like a slave, that's all!"

"Oh?" He raised his eyebrows. "And who is the slave driver, may I ask?"

"Well, I guess it's really not that bad," she relented. "It's just that life isn't fair. I get up at five o'clock and milk cows all morning. As soon as breakfast is over, the others go off to school and I get stuck coming out here to wash up this mess by myself. When I'm done, I go to the house again and work some more. Today I have to help houseclean the living room, and there's a book I wanted to read instead."

Jennifer stopped speaking and watched the driver connect the big hose to the outlet at the bottom of the milk tank.

"Don't you like working in the barn?" he inquired. "I know some girls that really enjoy it, especially when I come around."

The tone of his voice puzzled Jennifer, but it was soon forgotten. "It's not so much that I hate the barn," she said. "I don't mind the milking, and I like caring for the calves and watching them grow, especially when they do well. What I really mind is that on this place there's no time for anything but work."

"It does seem some folks get more than their share," he agreed. "Sounds as if you could be one of them."

Jennifer was almost ready to tell him her woes about having no time to embroider pillowcases or piece quilts as some of her friends did, when she realized that she was revealing her personal feelings to a strange man—a man to whom she had never said more than a friendly greeting before.

"I guess I'd better be going," she said as she turned to leave for the house.

"I'm about done here." The driver spoke in the same casual tone he had used throughout the conversation. "Don't you wash the tank as well? You'll have to come back out later if you don't stay to do it now."

Jennifer stopped with her hand on the doorknob. "If you're almost finished I might as well do it now."

A few moments later the driver left the milk house and soon he had the big tanker truck rolling down the lane. Jennifer watched him go, wondering how she could have been so free to share her troubles with him.

"Jennifer Martin," she rebuked herself firmly, "what ails you anyway? You know perfectly well that you have no business confiding to an ungodly man!"

Jennifer knew, yes. But a number of times throughout the day as she helped houseclean the living room, she thought of Ray and his sympathetic ear. Those thoughts warmed a stubborn streak in her spirit—a streak that rejoiced to know she was not alone in thinking she had a hard lot.

"Of course it won't happen again," she consoled herself. "I guess once won't do a lot of harm."

The milk truck continued to come to the farm every other day. Occasionally Jennifer was still in the milk house when it arrived. More often she was on her way to the house or already there when the tanker turned into their lane.

One Thursday morning, however, she was surprised by the roar of the truck motor just as she started to wash the milkers. It was eight-fifteen, and Jennifer wondered why he had come so early.

She went on about her work, looking up only briefly as Ray stepped into the milk house. She said a quick good morning in response to his greeting and continued with her work.

"So how's the little slave getting along this morning?" Ray inquired after he had fastened the hose to the outlet of the milk tank.

Jennifer noticed that he was watching her with his usual casual air, and in spite of her earlier determination not to, she was soon recounting her woes to his attentive ear.

Such occasions became more frequent. Neither Jennifer nor her parents were aware that about once each week Ray would alter his route, coming first to the Martin farm and going back later to the one he had bypassed, further up the road.

Jennifer did not mind, for she found in Ray a sympathetic confidant. More and more she enjoyed the few minutes they spent together in the milk house. The Spirit still reminded her that she had no business talking so freely to an ungodly man. The warnings of conscience lessened, however, as time went on. But deep down, Jennifer was aware that her soul was not finding rest.

Several months passed, and one morning Jennifer realized with a pang that she was actually hoping Ray would come before she was done washing milkers. She had never expected the day to come when she would look forward like this to the time she spent with him.

One morning just after school was finished in the spring, Jennifer's father called her aside after breakfast.

"Jennifer," he said, "Dale is out of school permanently now, so I plan to have him take over the milk house cleanup in the mornings. I don't think it's wise for a seventeen-year-old girl to spend as much time alone with the driver as you have these past few months. You may do it yet this morning, but starting tomorrow morning Dale will take care of that job."

Jennifer tried hard not to let her disappointment show. Never would she want Father to guess how she felt about Ray. As she walked to the milk house, she realized even more what he had come to mean to her, and how much she would miss visiting with him. "And now it's all over," she thought. "Unless I see him this morning, we may never meet again!"

She had just finished filling the sink with water when she heard the familiar rumble of the tanker truck coming in the lane.

A few moments later, Ray stepped through the milk house door. "Morning!" he greeted her cheerily. "How's my favorite slave getting on with her work?"

She looked up with a faint smile as she answered, "It looks as though I won't be washing milkers any longer."

"Not washing milkers!" He arched his eyebrows in a manner that had become familiar to her. "How come? I don't like to hear that!"

Jennifer went back to work as she replied, "Oh, Father says Dale will do it now since he's out of school."

"I guess our little milk house visits will come to an end then," Ray said. The clatter of the milkers in the sink muffled his steps, and Jennifer did not observe that he was walking slowly toward her as he spoke.

"Well, never mind," he consoled. "I think we can arrange something else." He slipped his arm around her waist and began to draw her to himself.

Jennifer jumped, soaking them both with sudsy water as the milker pail she had been washing splashed into the full sink. With sudden panic she realized the danger she had allowed herself to be trapped in. Without a word she turned and fled, dripping, to the house.

Mother looked up in astonishment as her daughter

burst into the kitchen, breathless from her dash across the yard. The entire front of her dress was soaked, and remnants of suds still clung to the front of her hair. Tears streamed down her cheeks, and she was sobbing half in remorse and half in fear.

"Why, Jennifer!" Mother exclaimed. "Whatever happened?"

Jennifer mopped her face with the skirt of her apron. "Oh, Mother! I didn't realize what I was getting into!" She went on to recount to her mother what had occurred.

Jennifer saw Mother's face turn pale as she told her story. "I'm going to call Father," she said when Jennifer was finished relating the account. "I think he ought to know this right away."

As Mother left the kitchen, Jennifer slowly rose from her chair and went to her room for dry clothing. When Father and Mother appeared, she was back and was peeling carrots that Mother had left in the sink.

"Jennifer," Father began, and his voice was trembling, "I guess I don't know how to begin to tell you how terrible I feel that I allowed this to happen. I should have put a stop to you and Ray being together long before this. We can really thank the Lord that He protected you in spite of my failure," he added.

Father was silent for a long time, then he went on. "I knew it wasn't the best arrangement, but someone had to clean up the milk house, and I didn't think I had time. I'm sorry—terribly sorry!"

Jennifer looked up through her tears. Her gaze met that of her father, and the rebellious spirit she had nurtured toward him for so long melted like a piece of plastic melts in a flame.

"Oh, Father, Mother, it was my fault!" she cried brokenly. "I knew I had no business telling him my troubles. But he was such an understanding listener, and I never dreamed it would lead to something like this." She paused and then added slowly, "I'm terribly sorry."

"I'm sure you are," agreed her father, "and so am I. My failure doesn't excuse yours completely, nor does yours excuse mine. I trust that by the grace of God none of my children will ever again have to learn any lesson in such a dangerous way. God helping me, I never want to allow myself to be so busy again that I would allow such a circumstance to exist.

"And now," he added, "I think we ought to get down on our knees and confess to the Lord that we're sorry for having failed Him as well as for having failed each other."

Jennifer's heart bubbled with thanksgiving that day as she went about her hitherto-unwelcome tasks. "God has been good to me," she told Mother. "I don't deserve the protection He has given."

Mother nodded. "Proverbs asks whether one can take fire into his bosom and his clothes not be burned," she said. "It also asks if one can go on hot coals and his feet not be burned."

"It surely applies, doesn't it," Jennifer agreed. "Only God's mercy saved me from the fire that was so near. I see it so clearly now. I was walking on coals."

Later that evening, while Father and Mother were relaxing on the porch swing, Jennifer went to them and asked, "Do you think I should make a confession of my overall rebellious attitude? Should I say something about it to the church? I've been thinking about it, and wonder if I shouldn't."

Father nodded slowly. "I've been thinking the same thing, Jennifer," he said. He hesitated and then went on. "In your case, almost everyone in the congregation has been aware of your problem with rebellious attitudes here at home. It would probably be good for both you and the congregation if you would make a public confession.

"That, however, isn't quite what I had in mind a moment ago when I said I'd been thinking the same thing. What I had in mind is that almost everyone is also aware that I've been so engrossed with making money that I've not taken the amount of time I should have to nurture and direct my children properly.

"We'll talk these matters over with the ministry, of course. At this point, though, I feel that each of us has a public confession to make."

A Little Fun

───•◆•───

THE COOL SHOWER HAD felt good to Aaron, who had been handling hay bales all day in the July heat, and he yawned heavily as he turned off the light beside his bed. "I'm too tired for devotions tonight," he thought. "I wouldn't get anything out of it if I tried."

"But this is the third time this week that you've been too tired." The voice of the Holy Spirit was gentle but persistent. "You know you need the nourishment of God's Word daily. You're establishing a pattern of neglect. When a Christian fails to feed on God's Word, he always substitutes with something of lesser value."

Aaron groaned. "Not tonight," he argued. "I'm too tired." He turned over and settled into his pillow. "I'll try real hard to read two chapters tomorrow."

By the time the busy crop season was over, Aaron had

established a habit of neglecting his devotions. He had also begun to develop an interest in reading material that was less than desirable—books that he had learned he could buy cheaply from the used books store in town.

As time went on, Aaron developed the habit of waiting until his younger brother, Myron, was asleep and then bringing out his book and reading far into the night. One night late in November he yawned as he slid the book he had been reading under the mattress and turned off the light. Even with the slower winter schedule, he needed some rest. Myron had been sleeping for hours already. "I sure wanted to finish this book yet tonight," Aaron thought as he turned over. But with having to wait until Myron was asleep before getting started, well...

His thoughts trailed off as he nestled down into the covers. "There's nothing like a mystery thriller to take a fellow's mind off his own ideas," he thought as he drifted off to sleep. "If I could just get Myron interested in mysteries, then I wouldn't have to worry that he'd tell Father and Mother about my books."

Aaron knew that Myron was too interested in spiritual things to be easily led into reading mystery novels. But surely, he thought, if he would go at it right, he could get Myron to come around.

Aaron followed up on his plans, beginning with interesting animal stories that Myron enjoyed. Gradually, the emphasis shifted, however, and by spring, Myron was neglecting his Bible study in favor of Aaron's exciting reading materials.

Six months after Aaron first began to woo Myron away from his spiritual interests, the two boys stayed home to take care of the farm while their parents took a trip to visit relatives in a distant area. When they had finished their work one evening, Aaron showed Myron a tape he had borrowed from a neighbor.

"I don't know," Myron answered guardedly. "What would Father and Mother say?"

"Oh, come on!" Aaron scoffed. "What does it matter what our parents think? They're a thousand miles away. Here's our chance to have a little fun!"

"But we might get caught," Myron replied.

The sliver of fear in his brother's voice did not escape Aaron's attention. "Caught! Yeah! We might get caught! We might get caught some evening reading too. What would you do then?"

"Stuff the book under the covers, just like we've agreed already," Myron replied. "And start talking about some spiritual subject, such as the meaning of feet washing, that Father would be pleased to hear us discussing. We've already agreed on that!"

"Yeah. Well, who's going to catch us now? There's no one on this whole farm but the two of us. If anyone should come along, Rover will howl as usual. Come on, sissy. Don't be a scaredy-cat! When are you going to loosen up and have a little fun?"

Several months later, after Bishop Peter Miller had

finished the announcements one Sunday morning, he stood silent for a long moment behind the pulpit. At last he spoke.

"Brethren and sisters, my heart is heavy this morning." He hesitated, then went on. "Two young men from among us have lost their way with the Lord. They are not interested in repenting of their sinful practices. Aaron Peters and Myron Peters hereby forfeit their membership in the congregation, and each of them shall be held in excommunicated status until such time as he repents and is reconciled to the Lord of the church.

"Let us pray earnestly for them, and go out of our way to demonstrate our love," the bishop went on. "Their souls are precious to the Lord; may they be so to us also."

Aaron and Myron continued to attend church services after their excommunication, but several months went by and neither of them gave any evidence of repentance. The busy season began on the farm again. Aaron felt very tired, but as long as he was driving a tractor, he got along all right. He no longer lay awake at night reading, though. He was too tired.

As haying season neared, he began to dread handling bales. What, he wondered, had happened to his strength? A young man like him should have energy to spare, and here he was getting tired just driving a tractor.

"Take it easy for a few days," Father advised when Aaron told him how weary he always felt. "Rest most of the time for the remainder of the week and see what happens. If that doesn't help, we'll take you to Dr. Brownlee. You do look pale lately. Mother noticed it, and I did too."

So Aaron took it easy. He had, in fact, been taking it more easy than usual for quite a while already. He had not read in bed for several months, so he was getting more sleep than he had been used to during the previous two years.

But the more he rested, the more the hours seemed to drag. Everything he did took a great deal of effort—a strength that somehow he no longer had. At the end of the week he was almost more tired than he had been before.

"I suppose we might as well try it," he agreed when Father suggested an appointment with the family doctor. "Maybe Dr. Brownlee will find what's wrong. There certainly has to be something!"

Dr. Brownlee examined Aaron thoroughly. "I'll have to take blood tests before I can tell you anything for sure," was all he would say about his findings. "Until they come back on Thursday afternoon, continue as you've been, getting lots of rest."

The doctor's receptionist called Aaron's home on Thursday afternoon. "Dr. Brownlee wants both you and your husband to come with Aaron first thing tomorrow morning," she requested when Mother answered the phone.

"Could the appointment be put off until Monday?" Mother inquired. "We have a lot of hay down and it should go into the barn tomorrow. And of course the doctor isn't in on Saturday."

"Dr. Brownlee said first thing Friday morning," the receptionist replied. "I'm sure he wouldn't have been so specific if it wasn't important."

"Well, I guess we can arrange it then," Mother said slowly.

Aaron came into the room just then. "Could arrange what?"

But Mother shook her head. "I'll have to talk to Father."

Early the next morning they were in Dr. Brownlee's examination room. Aaron felt as though a needle was shooting jets of tension all through his body. Unless the doctor came soon, he thought, he would scream—would explode—would, well, would what? What was the matter with him? It must be serious. Otherwise the doctor would not have insisted on having both of his parents here. After all, he was nineteen years old, almost twenty.

He tried to sort out the various muscular abnormalities he had heard of in his lifetime. Might his getting weaker all the time mean that he had an incurable disease? Would he become an invalid? What was the matter with him anyhow?

A gentle tap sounded on the door of the examination room, and the doctor entered. The grave look on his face drove fear deep into Aaron's being.

Dr. Brownlee sat behind his desk, folding and unfolding his hands. He thumbed through the sheaf of papers he had brought with him. He adjusted his glasses, and then he cleared his throat.

The knots in Aaron's stomach twisted tighter than before.

"We have the results of your tests," the doctor began at last. He did not look up. "You have a very serious illness…"

The words trailed off, and still the doctor did not look up. Aaron stared at him, willing him to look at him, to make eye contact, to act like the Dr. Brownlee he had known all his life.

"Aaron." At last the doctor raised his face to meet his patient's gaze. "Do you have any idea what leukemia means?"

The intravenous drip of fear surged to a rushing torrent. Raw, jagged, numbing terror swirled through his brain. The universe spiraled away into a suffocating horror. Yes, he knew what leukemia meant. Death.

One Sunday morning two months later, Bishop Peter Miller addressed the congregation with deep feeling. "I'm sure we are all aware of the events of the past months in Aaron Peters' life," he began. "I think we have accepted the fact that Aaron won't be in this world much longer. This brings us sorrow, especially for his family, who will miss him the most.

"But there's an aspect of triumph in Aaron's story too, for through the outworkings of his illness he has again found Jesus precious to his soul."

For a long moment the bishop stood there silent, then

at last he went on. "It is with great joy that we reinstate Brother Aaron as a member in good standing in this congregation. He is too ill to be here, but I have a written statement from him that I want to read at this time."

Several months later, Aaron lay very still on his hospital bed. He knew his life was almost over, that soon now he would go home.

"Lord, You know how happy I am that You brought me back to Yourself," he prayed silently. "Thank you for continuing to call me during the months when I failed to respond. Father, help me to be faithful through whatever I must yet suffer before You take me home. Use my life to help others find You.

"Especially speak to Myron, Lord. You know how I urged him to stray from You. Oh, how I wish I had never done it! If only I could go back, I'd surely encourage him to follow You instead."

Tears rolled down Aaron's hollow cheeks as he interceded for his wayward brother. "Lord, if I can reach him in any way, I'm willing to suffer whatever it might take to bring him back to You."

Six days later, Bishop Peter Miller stood beside Aaron's coffin. "Well, Myron, Aaron is at rest now—home with the Lord," he said tenderly to the young man standing beside his brother's body. "Aaron suffered much the last while here, but his pain is all over now." The bishop lowered his voice so that only Myron could hear.

"The last thing he said to me was, 'I wish so much that Myron would come back to God and the church. I feel so wretched for having lured him away!'

"I know your brother would have rejoiced beyond anything we can imagine if he could have lived to see that happen, Myron," Brother Peter went on. "Wouldn't you like to prepare to meet Aaron in glory?"

Myron turned his gaze away and shrugged. "Maybe someday," he answered. "For now, I want to have a little fun."

Dilemma in Dutch

EVELYN USUALLY ENJOYED VISITING with the other sisters at sewing circle the first Tuesday of each month. But today it was all so different. She bit her lip determinedly as she pushed her needle through the seam that crossed the line of quilting in front of her fingers. The other women sitting around the quilt with her were laughing and talking merrily, but Evelyn had never felt so alone.

She snipped the thread at the end of her line of stitching and knotted the part that was left in the needle, preparing to start another row of quilting. The six sisters around her laughed again, and Evelyn bit her lip harder. But the discomfort seemed only to encourage the tears that she knew now were almost ready to spill over.

She wished desperately that baby June would wake up and cry. That would give her a good excuse to get away from the others without anyone noticing that she had a problem.

But her baby did not cooperate, and the unintelligible chatter around her continued until she could bear it no longer. "Lord, help me to escape without anyone observing my problem," she prayed silently. She pushed her chair back quietly and turned away from the quilt. The tears spilled over as she walked toward the bathroom at the opposite end of the house from the bedroom where her infant was still sleeping.

She noticed that the babble continued uninterrupted, and she was glad for the assurance that no one had noticed anything amiss with her. "Thank you, Father," she said silently. "But where do I go from here now? What should I do next? Lord, You know how very left out I feel.

"It probably shouldn't bother me," she continued. "But it does anyway. I know the sisters don't intend to hurt me. I'm sure that no one thought this through very well before they asked me when Elvin dropped me off here this morning whether I'd mind if for just this one day they'd not speak anything but Pennsylvania Dutch.

"What could I have answered, Lord? Should I have been open enough to admit that I did suspect it would make me feel left out? Didn't they already know that? How would any one of them feel if she were the one who didn't understand anything that was being said?"

Evelyn wished she had a vehicle there, but Elvin had brought her when he was on his way to work, and he would not be back to pick her up for another three hours. How could she stand it that much longer? Even the prayer at dinnertime had been in a language she knew nothing of.

She applied a cold washcloth to her tear-stained face. "I don't want to embarrass them by bringing attention to how I feel, Father," she prayed. "But what can I do?"

A look in the mirror confirmed her suspicion that anyone who so much as glanced at her would know right away that something was amiss.

Just then, baby June started crying. But now Evelyn hoped that she would settle back down. For the group of women gathered around the quilt was between her and her baby. She would have to go past them to reach her child. Surely June would soon go back to sleep!

It soon became obvious, however, that June was in no mood to sleep without attention first. The demands from the bedroom became more and more insistent. With a helpless glance in the mirror, Evelyn turned the doorknob and stepped into the hall.

The babble of voices in the room beyond continued. Noticing that the infant had stopped crying, she hesitated a moment, hoping for a few minutes' further respite. She was almost ready to return to the bathroom when Sister Norma stepped through the doorway from the living room into the hallway where Evelyn was standing. The older woman had baby June in her arms.

"This little lass was calling for her..." Norma stopped

in mid-sentence. "Why, Evelyn, what's wrong?"

The loving concern that Evelyn saw on the older woman's face unleashed her tears again, and she struggled desperately for self-control.

"It's all right," she sobbed. "I'll be fine in a moment." She mopped at the tears with the back of her hand as she spoke. She was determined not to tell Norma or anyone else what was bothering her.

"If it would help to share with someone…"

Norma's kind offer and straightforward gaze almost disarmed her, but Evelyn shook her head.

"Oh, Evelyn, how could we have?" A horrified expression dawned on Norma's face as the nature of the younger sister's problem registered in her mind. "I'm terribly sorry. I never gave a thought to how we were making you feel. I'm sure no one else did either. You must be feeling dreadfully left out!"

Evelyn nodded miserably and the tears began afresh. Now everyone at the quilt would find out how their thoughtlessness had hurt her. How much she wanted to keep her feelings to herself. But Norma had guessed.

Evelyn's tears of frustration on her own behalf turned to tears of remorse at the thought that others would feel badly when they learned about her problem.

Norma waited while Evelyn composed herself.

"What will I do now?" Evelyn was still wiping tears as she asked. "I didn't want anyone to know. They didn't mean to hurt me, I know…"

Norma smiled. "All right," she said. "You and I have a secret." She hugged Evelyn with the arm that was not holding the baby. "I'm terribly sorry we were so thoughtless, and I can assure you that it never will happen again. To save you from embarrassment, I'll not say anything about your feelings until sometime when you aren't present. I can't understand how we could have been so heartless. It was cruel indeed to ask you the way we did. After all, what else could you have said?"

"I certainly don't hold anything against anyone," Evelyn answered. "You didn't think it through, I'm sure." She reached for her baby. "After all, you asked me if I'd mind. I didn't know when I said it was all right just how much I really would mind. And it wasn't so bad at first, but as hour after hour went on with you all laughing and enjoying yourselves, I couldn't help feeling left out."

"It won't happen again!" Norma repeated emphatically. "Now, you make yourself comfortable there in the office and feed your little one. And meanwhile, I'll do my best to see to it that by the time you get back to the living room, everybody will be speaking English!"

Beyond My Expectations

SWIRLS OF DRIED LEAVES rustled to the ground and a squirrel foraged for acorns under the oak tree in the yard. The intervals between passing vehicles were punctuated occasionally by the cacophony of Canada geese as they winged southward overhead.

Free, Roger thought, and there was a trace of sarcasm mixed with envy, almost of resentment, as he reflected on the word. Driven by instinct to be sure, but nevertheless free. Free to come and go when and where they pleased.

He gripped the arms of his wheelchair. Roger Norris would never be free again. The accident a year ago had seen to it that he would never come and go as he pleased. Until Father and Mother came home from work, he was not even free to get off this porch and search the sky for the undulating chains of great gray birds whose plaintive honking haunted the October afternoon.

The wild geese had always been special to Roger, and he felt more than a trace of sadness now as he recalled the drowsy afternoons of autumns past when, lying on his back among the fallen leaves, his gaze followed wedge after wedge of honkers down the invisible flyways of the sky.

But now ... well, at least he could hear them. He still had the usual senses, or most of them. From his chest downward, he felt nothing. And that so-called sixth sense, the awareness of position, was missing in his lower limbs.

He remembered now that someday he would be eternally free. No more sorrow, no more tears, no more pain—and no wheelchair either. "Lord, I'm sorry I allowed myself to be discontented again," he prayed. "I should be thankful for my handicap. If it hadn't been for the accident, I might never have met the Martin family and never have come to know Jesus as my Savior."

The Lord had used his hospital experience in the big city to bring the Martin family into his life, and with them his first acquaintance with Christianity. The Martins' son, John, had an accident the day after Roger had his. Now both boys had returned to their homes after several weeks in the same hospital room. John's health had been fully restored. Roger was a paraplegic. Mindful of the therapist's instructions, he hitched himself up with his elbows to change his position. "Your body no longer tells you when to move, so now you have to tell it when to move instead," the therapist had emphasized over and over. "We must avoid pressure sores at any cost."

"If only I could find a job as easily as I can avoid pressure sores!" Roger mused. He knew he would never fulfill his youthful dream of being a diesel mechanic. But what could he do?

"Help me to wait patiently for whatever You have for me, Lord," he prayed. "Help me not to allow myself to be bitter about my handicap. You know how the time drags and how I long to be doing something productive. You also know the trials I face with my ungodly parents. Lord, help them to understand my need for a position that's consistent with the requirements of the Scriptures."

Four different jobs that it seemed he could have done had come to his attention since he finished school in the spring. He had tried each of them briefly, but his limitations had been too restrictive. Then just the past week, he had refused a cashier position in a variety store nearby. With the accommodations the owners were prepared to make for him, Roger was sure he could have done the work in spite of his handicap.

"And you turned it down because you'd have to sell radios and jewelry!" his father had stormed. "I can't see why you have to be so particular!"

Explanations did not help. Was it worth the constant hassle with his parents to live up to what he knew was right? Or might he just as well give in and pretend he had never learned of anything better? If only his parents would find the Lord Jesus as their Savior!

"Help me to be patient, Lord," he prayed. "Draw them to Yourself. You know how they need You. Help me to be faithful too, and to be a good witness to them.

"You know how much I long for a scriptural church to attend," he went on. "Work it all out as it pleases You, Father."

Quick footfalls on the sidewalk indicated the approach of the mailman. A card, a letter, or a postcard, often from someone he did not know but who was nevertheless a brother or sister in the Lord, reached him almost every day. He waited now, eager to see what might come today.

The Martin family made a point of visiting him every two weeks. The other members of their congregation had committed themselves not only to pray for him but also to write regularly. There was no church similar to the Martins' anywhere near Roger's home, therefore the brethren felt a very real concern to provide fellowship for this fledgling Christian.

"Morning, young man! Beautiful day. Letter for you as usual. Must be nice to be so popular! I don't get a letter every day." With a grin the postman dropped the day's bundle of mail into Roger's lap and was gone.

Roger shuffled through the assortment of envelopes and the advertising brochures. Sure enough, there was one letter addressed to him. The return address puzzled him, however, being from a distant state. He slid his pocketknife blade through the fold at the top of the envelope, wondering who it was from and what it might contain.

Dear Brother Roger,

Greetings in Jesus' Name. Isn't it wonderful to know Him? Even though we don't know each other, we're both a part of His family. And we both know John Martin. In fact, I'm his uncle.

John's family visited us a few weeks ago. They told us how you found the Lord in the hospital. They also told of your difficulty finding work. It's over a thousand miles out here, so I was hesitant to contact you about working for us. But now we feel the Lord wants us to make this offer.

We operate a business machine repair service. Our volume of work is increasing constantly, and since our children are all in school they can't help much. If this interests you, we would want you to live here with our family.

Please pray about it and let us know what you think.

Your Brother in Christ,
James Martin

"Lord, is this Your answer?" Roger's fingers trembled as he read the letter again. A family who would give him not only a job but also a Christian home. There would be a scriptural church where he could go regularly.

Repairing business machines would be much different from diesel engine work, but maybe he could learn... His thoughts turned somersaults over each other as he considered the pros and cons of the offer.

What would Father and Mother say about his moving so far and living with a Christian family? "Lord, You'll have to work it out for me," he whispered. "You can prepare the way if this is Your will. You know how much I want to do this, Lord!"

. . .

One afternoon six months later, the bell jingled above the door of the repair shop where Roger was working on a calculator. Two men stepped into the building, and Roger looked up from his work.

"Well, John Martin!" he exclaimed at the sight of his friend. "And Brother Paul too!" Roger pushed his wheelchair away from the specially designed workbench that John's Uncle James had helped him build. "This is wonderful! I didn't know you were coming! How long do you plan to stay?"

His visitors greeted him warmly. "We hoped you wouldn't find our coming unpleasant anyhow," John said, and he was smiling as he spoke.

A happy visit followed, and a few minutes later John's uncle joined them. "Well, Roger, how do you like your surprise?" he asked. "Aunt Katie and I expected you to be overjoyed."

"He is," John said. "He could hardly talk straight when we first arrived. He says it was because he was so glad to see us. We're glad to see him too."

The two days that John and his father stayed seemed almost to fly by. "So you like it here?" John asked as he watched his friend take a calculator apart on the last afternoon of their visit.

Roger nodded. "I sure do! I can't think of anything I'd rather do, now that I've learned the trade. It was frustrating at times the first while, of course."

"The accommodations work all right?" John asked next.

"Yes. With this special workbench and the ramps your uncle built for me to get around on the grounds, everything is so convenient it's hard for me to believe all the things I can do. And this electric wheelchair lets me go up and down ramps by myself. You can't imagine what it would be like to have to ask for help every time you wanted to go up or down a couple of steps. The arrangement here is really wonderful!"

"You don't get homesick?" John inquired.

Roger shook his head. "With your four lively cousins, I don't have time," he answered. "Your uncle and aunt have gone far out of their way to make me feel like a son here in their home too. And the church is an even greater blessing than I ever could have imagined.

"From the time I first found the Lord, I thought it would be nice to attend a church like yours," he went on. "I often tried to imagine what that would be like. But the blessings here have gone far beyond my expectations. The accident was a hard experience, and my handicap made me bitter for a while. But looking at it from where I am now, has certainly been worth everything I've been through to know that I'm in the center of God's will."

Love Will Make It Possible

"SISTER ROSE MENTIONED THAT Darrin and Ruby are coming for a visit soon," Mother informed Father and Sharon on the way home from church. "They'll be here for three days. Ruby and Grace were such good friends. They spent a lot of time in each other's homes the last several years when they were both teaching too. I'm looking forward to seeing Ruby again. She almost seems like one of our family."

"Nancy told me about their visit too," Sharon agreed. "They're sure excited. They haven't seen Darrins since their wedding four months ago."

"I suppose we'll be just as excited when we get word that Allen and Grace are coming to visit us," Father observed. Allen and Grace had been married one week after Darrin and Ruby were.

"We won't see them nearly this soon, though," Sharon said. "They won't come as often as Darrin and Ruby do either. Darrins are just 400 miles away; Allen and Grace have more than 2,000 miles."

"That's true," Mother agreed. "Traveling is costly, so I don't expect we'll see them for at least a year."

Father and Mother chatted on, but Sharon's thoughts were elsewhere. Why did it have to be her sister who lived so far away?

After dinner, Mother and Sharon washed the dishes. Sharon plopped a clean bowl into the drainer. "Mother, could we invite Darrin and Ruby over while they're here?" she asked.

"I think we could," Mother answered. "They'll be in the area for three days. We could ask them at least. Grace isn't at home, of course, but Ruby was here so often the last few years that she might want to come anyhow, just to see us."

"Let's ask them for Saturday supper," Sharon suggested.

"I'll see what Father thinks," Mother answered. "If it's all right with him, I'll call them sometime Friday afternoon."

Mother made the call to Ruby's home on Friday. "Thank you for the invitation," Ruby said. "I'm sure we'd enjoy being there, but we'll need to talk it over here first. I'll let you know shortly."

A few minutes later the telephone rang. "I see,"

Mother said after she had listened for a moment. "Well, maybe some other time, then. Meanwhile, we'll look forward to seeing you at church on Sunday. Good-bye."

"Ruby said she and Darrin would like to come," Mother explained. "But her family prefers that they stay there all the time."

"But Saturday supper would take less than two hours!" Sharon exclaimed. "Two hours doesn't seem like much out of three whole days. And Darrin and Ruby want to come. I don't think it's fair that her family won't allow it!"

"Ruby didn't say they wouldn't allow them to come," Father said. "I believe it was that they would prefer for them to stay there. Darrin and Ruby decided, and we must be satisfied."

Sharon said no more. But she was not satisfied, and she could not forget how unfair it was. *If only Allens would have decided to live here instead of where his family is, then Grace wouldn't be more than 2,000 miles away,* she thought. *Maybe then I wouldn't mind so much being the only child left here at home.*

.   .   .

"Allen and Grace are coming for a visit at last!" Sharon's voice quivered with excitement as she shared the news with Nancy. "They'll be here for only four days, though, and it's been well over a year since their wedding. That's when we saw them last."

"I get excited when Darrin and Ruby are coming to see us too," Nancy said. "And they've been here three times already. We went there once too, and stayed for a whole week. Of course 400 miles isn't nearly as much as 2,000."

Allen and Grace arrived late Thursday evening. The family was still at the breakfast table on Friday morning when the phone rang. "It's for Grace," Father said after he had answered.

Sharon listened. Allen and Grace had just arrived. Who would want to talk to them so soon?

"We'll discuss it and let you know," Grace said into the receiver. Soon she had finished the call. "It was Ruby's mother," she explained. "They want Allen and me to go there for Sunday afternoon, including dinner, of course. It would be nice, but we have only four days altogether and we do want to spend some time with Grandpa Bylers."

"I think we'll be busy enough, given the little time we have to spend in the area," Allen agreed. "Tell them we appreciate the invitation, but we feel that for this time at least we'd like to spend the time we have with your family."

"And we'll see them at church," Grace added. "That's better than not seeing them at all." She went to the phone.

Grace shook her head a few minutes later as she returned to the table. "They just won't take no for an answer," she said. "I didn't know what more to say, so I said we'd talk it over again. I even suggested they could come here, but they wouldn't do that either."

Allen looked puzzled. "What do you suggest, Father?" he asked. "I hardly know what to say..." His voice trailed off.

"You and Grace will have to decide," Father said. "I don't know either why they're so insistent."

At least they could have invited us to come along! Sharon fumed inwardly on the way home from church on Sunday. *How can they think this is fair when they refused to let Darrins come to our house for two hours? And now Nancy says that no matter how often Darrins come, they want them to stay at their place all the time.*

"Well, I sure hope they have a good time!" she said aloud. She felt even worse after having voiced her feelings, and Father and Mother's silence made her more miserable yet. "At least they could reprove me for my unforgiving attitude," she thought.

"I know I shouldn't feel this way," she added lamely. "But it's just that it's so dreadfully unfair!"

"I think I understand how you feel," Father replied. "And you're right. It isn't fair. But we have to leave that between Ruby's family and the Lord. Allen and Grace finally decided to go because they didn't know what else to do. Given the circumstances, I think they made the wisest choice."

"And we want to learn from this too," Mother added. "It has already helped me to see that at times I've not been as considerate of other people's feelings as I should have been."

"Love makes it possible for us to accommodate ourselves to things that are unfair," Father added. "Meanwhile, we don't want to let this disappointment ruin our enjoyment of the time we do have to spend with Allen and Grace. If we're nursing resentment, we won't enjoy their visit as much as we otherwise could now, and our memories of it won't be as pleasant either."

"I know you're right," Sharon agreed a little wistfully. "I just wish I could accept it as calmly as you do. I don't want to feel bitter toward Ruby's family either. Pray for me." Tears squeezed out as she finished speaking.

"The Lord will bless you for such an attitude," Father commended. "It won't always be easy, but by God's grace you can do it. Mother and I will pray for you, of course. And God will bless you as you yield your feelings to Him."

Many times in the weeks that followed, the evil one brought Sharon memories of how unfair Ruby's family had been. But she soon learned that the joy of the Lord could not dwell in her heart when she allowed herself to harbor any traces of resentment.

"I'm so glad God has given me victory," she confided to Mother some time later. "But it didn't come until I admitted that I couldn't do it myself and then asked the Lord to put genuine love in my heart for all of Ruby's family. And Father was right. I have much sweeter memories of Allen and Grace's visit now that resentment isn't there."

Not Like Uncle Elwood!

PRAYER MEETING WAS OVER, and the congregation was making good use of the opportunity to fellowship with each other.

"Good evening, Sister Mary Lou." Calvin smiled as he spoke to his pastor's wife. "I'm sorry to hear that your mother isn't well."

A cheery conversation between Calvin and the pastor's wife followed, with her mother's health being but one of several items discussed. When Sister Mary Lou turned aside to visit with the other women, Calvin looked around thoughtfully.

"Let me see," he thought. "Who else were the prayer requests for this evening? Oh, yes, there's Sister Laura. Her brother and his wife are leaving for the mission field next week."

"Good evening, Sister Laura," he said aloud. He waited a moment to get her attention. "I'm sure you're going to miss your brother and his family."

Once again, a friendly visit ensued, and before long Calvin saw his father and the younger boys in the family disappearing through the back door of the church house.

Calvin slipped unnoticed past a group of brethren who were visiting together and hurried toward the parking lot. Long strides brought him to the driver's side of his family's vehicle just in time to help his Aunt Lucy into the car that was parked beside theirs.

Crippled as she was, his mother's oldest sister had made her way through the snowy parking lot by herself. Now she was struggling with the door latch on her car, hardly able to open it with her deformed fingers.

"Here, Auntie," Calvin said as he reached for the door latch. "Let me get that for you.

"Take good care of yourself," he added as he tucked her coat out of the way and closed the door. "I'll be glad to let Uncle Elwood know you're out here. You'll get cold if you wait very long."

"Oh, never mind," his aunt answered quickly. "I just got tired and thought I'd come to the car. I'm sure Uncle Elwood will be here any minute."

As Calvin slid behind the steering wheel of the family vehicle, he thought to himself that Uncle Elwood could help Aunt Lucy a great deal more than he did. Glancing sideways at his father, he said, "It almost seems that the more crippled Aunt Lucy gets, the more Uncle Elwood ignores her needs!"

Father nodded slowly. "It's sad, isn't it?" Father turned the conversation to other channels, and soon the family was home.

One Tuesday morning a few weeks later, Calvin made a trip to town to do errands for various members of his family. His first stop was at the hardware store where he bought a can of paint.

"We can always tell when spring's coming by the amount of paint we sell," the saleslady commented as she rang up his purchase.

"And by the number of men who get sent to town to buy it because the women are too busy housecleaning!" Calvin quipped with a chuckle. A friendly conversation ensued.

A stop at the post office to purchase stamps came next. Again the salesperson was a woman. And again a witty remark from Calvin set the wheels of conversation into motion.

After leaving the post office, Calvin went to the implement dealership to pick up cultivator parts.

"So where's my uncle this morning?" he greeted the young man who came to wait on him at the parts counter.

"Who? Elwood? Is he your uncle?"

Calvin thought he caught a note of disdain in the man's voice. He nodded. "That's right. Not that I needed to talk to him about anything. I just expected to say hello while I was here."

"Not today. He's off Wednesdays. Probably he's downtown somewhere entertaining the ladies with his witty little stories, the same as he does here the other five days of the business week. There's never a woman comes in here but what Elwood has to be the one to help her. He's all business when he deals with men, but you ought to see his face light up when he talks to women!"

Calvin felt his own face grow warm, and he finished his business as quickly as he could.

The grocery store was not busy when he got there, and the little shopping he had to do did not take long. As he carried his purchases to the pickup, a familiar laugh rang across the parking lot.

"That's Uncle Elwood," he realized. "Likely they do their grocery shopping on his day off." A quick scan of the vehicles in the parking lot revealed his uncle's car on the opposite side from where he had parked his pickup.

He dumped his groceries hurriedly onto the pickup seat and turned toward his relatives. He would take time for a little chat with them.

As he slammed the door of the pickup shut, a woman's laugh came from the same direction his uncle's had, but he knew it was not Aunt Lucy's.

Slowing his steps, he surveyed the situation. His uncle was standing with the driver's door of his car open, and was carrying on a bantering conversation with a woman

Calvin did not know. On the passenger side of the vehicle, his crippled aunt was trying desperately to wrestle her bags of groceries out of the shopping cart and into the back seat of the car.

A surge of bitterness swept over Calvin when he saw how she was struggling, and he broke into a run.

"Here, Aunt Lucy. You need help with those heavy packages!" He knew his voice was unnecessarily loud, but right now he wanted Uncle Elwood to hear. He wanted the woman with whom he was talking to hear as well.

His aunt looked up with eyes full of relief and gratitude as Calvin's strong arms took the bundle from her hands. "Thank you, Calvin," she said quietly. "I could have managed, but it's easier for you than it is for me. Thank you!"

The gentleness and humility of Aunt Lucy's tone rebuked Calvin more than any words might have done, and it was a somewhat subdued nephew who helped her into the car and closed the door. Without a backward glance at his uncle, who was still engrossed in his conversation with the unknown woman, Calvin turned on his heel and clattered his aunt's empty shopping cart across the parking lot to the store.

Calvin wondered as he went whether, if no one would have come along to help her, his uncle would have stood there joking with that strange woman, whoever she was, until Aunt Lucy had taken the cart back by herself.

When the younger children were in bed that evening,

Calvin told his parents the story of his encounter with his uncle and aunt.

Mother nodded sadly when he was done. "We didn't know either that it was quite that bad," she said. "Lucy never says anything about it, of course. But our own eyes tell us some things along the way. However, I guess I've never seen them in town."

Father sighed. "I think Lucy feels that she deserves the type of husband she has," he said.

Mother nodded again. "When we were all young people years ago, your Uncle Elwood was considered by many of the girls in our congregation to be the most desirable young man in the group. He was popular with all the young folks, being very much at ease with boys and girls alike."

"That's right," Father agreed. "In fact, Elwood was more likely to visit with the women after church services than with the men. He had a quick wit about him, and almost everyone enjoyed his entertaining ways. Of course, I don't know why he favored entertaining the women rather than spending his time with the men."

"Many of the other girls were more than a little jealous when Elwood singled your Aunt Lucy out of the group," Mother said. "Lucy was pleased with her catch, of course. And none of us realized then where Elwood's charming ways with the ladies would lead him as time went on."

"It's only during the past few years that Mother and I started to see the outcome of that type of personality flaw as it grew to maturity," Father said. "In fact, I think Elwood is better able to hold the women's attention now than he was when he was younger."

"During the first years of their marriage, he did pay more attention to Lucy," Mother said. "But as time went on, it seemed that she turned out to be too quiet for him, and she just sort of got lost in the shuffle. He still lives with her, of course. But it seems that more and more he lives in a fantasy world where she doesn't even exist."

Father sighed. "I've been wondering the last while whether there wouldn't be some way of bringing this type of problem to the attention of our young people without exposing Elwood specifically. So far, I've never figured out how to do it. Of course the time will come, unless Elwood changes, when the church will have to address his failure."

"It's an object lesson we would all do well to take heed to," Mother said. "And some of us seem to need it more than others."

She was quiet then, but Calvin could feel something unusual in her expression.

"Calvin, Son," Father said slowly after a moment, "Mother and I have been asking the Lord for some time now to make an opportunity for us to help you see where you have some of the same problem that Uncle Elwood does, though it's not nearly as bad as his."

Calvin gazed first at his father and then at his mother. "Me?" he said blankly. "Me like Uncle Elwood. I don't know what you mean!"

"I'm sure you don't, Son," Father agreed. "As I said, I was watching for an opportunity to point it out to you. Your encounter with Elwood in town has made it easy for you to see for yourself what your uncle is like.

"But that's only half the story," Father continued. "The other half is up to you, Son. I'm confident that you never want to be like Uncle Elwood. The point is that thirty-five years ago, I'm sure Elwood didn't want to be like he is today either."

"He really did love Aunt Lucy, I'm sure," Mother said. "But he was just so used to being friendly to everyone that he probably didn't even realize when he stopped caring about her as much as he ought to have."

"And now in his older years, that attitude has gone to seed," Father added. "Not that it was wrong for him to ever talk to women, by any means. But it was wrong for him to give them so much attention."

Dumbfounded, Calvin listened as his father went on. Only the obvious love and concern in his parents' manners and voices kept him from asserting his own innocence. How could anyone possibly think that there was any danger of his ever being like Uncle Elwood?

"Think and pray about it, Son," Father concluded. "Make a mental note to observe who you spend most of your time with after church."

"It might help you to observe who you most enjoy conversations with when you occasionally go to town too," Mother added. "I noticed the other week when you and I went together that it seemed easy for you to joke and laugh with the salesladies. Try to keep an eye on yourself and see whether there might be a point to what we're saying. I too am sure you never want to be like your Uncle Elwood."

"You know we haven't said all this to be hard on you," Father said. He put his hand on Calvin's shoulder as he spoke. "We're eager for you to experience the very best the Lord has for you, both now and in the future. So think and pray about it, and let us know what you discover as you monitor yourself."

A very subdued Calvin headed toward his bedroom a few minutes later. "Thank you for caring," he said quietly. "And thank you for sharing with me like this. I can't see it yet, but I'll try hard to be honest in my observations from here on."

As he walked down the hall, the picture of his uncle and aunt in the grocery story parking lot came vividly to his mind. He could almost hear his uncle's hearty laughter and the responding giggle of the strange woman he was talking to.

The memory of dear Aunt Lucy's struggle with the groceries again brought a surge of bitterness, but this time the tang of self-righteousness that had accompanied that attitude earlier in the day was completely missing. In the light of his parents' warnings, perhaps he had better spend his time monitoring himself.

As he prepared for bed, Calvin determined to take

his parents' warning seriously, even though he could see no reason for their concern. And then the conversation he had had with the hardware store salesclerk earlier that morning came to his mind, and after that he was not quite as sure as he had been that there could not be anything to the things his parents had said.

But still, he certainly was not like Uncle Elwood—was he? "I'll start tomorrow evening at prayer meeting," he determined to himself. "I'll make a point of staying completely with the men at least for that time. I won't talk to the women or girls at all."

The following evening, as the family drifted away from the table after their bedtime snack, Calvin waited until the other children had all left the kitchen.

"Father, Mother," he said quietly, "I'm beginning to think that maybe you were more right than I would have believed. I went to the service this evening with my mind made up that this time I wouldn't talk to any of the sisters after the service was over. I wanted to prove to myself how easy that would be—to show that I most certainly was not as fond of talking to women as my uncle is."

Calvin hesitated, but his parents waited in silence, and a moment later he went on.

"It didn't go the way I thought it would," he admitted slowly. "Twice, in spite of my firm resolve, I caught myself not only speaking casually to one of the sisters, but actually singling one out for conversation in preference to the men!"

"I'm glad you shared this with us, Son," Father replied. "It's so much easier for any of us to overcome our weaknesses when we confront them openly and confess them to other people."

"There's nothing wrong with talking to one or another of the sisters occasionally," Mother added. "Our concern is that you seem to prefer them to the men when you have a choice."

"That's right," Father agreed. "Moreover, you seem to derive a greater degree of enjoyment and satisfaction from conversations with women than from those with men. For your own sake, you'd do well to cultivate a greater openness with the men and boys, and to practice more reserve with the women and girls."

Calvin nodded slowly. "After seeing what has happened to Uncle Elwood and Aunt Lucy, I surely have much reason to take your advice seriously," he said humbly. "I hope to have a wife of my own someday, and I certainly don't want to treat her the way Uncle Elwood treats Aunt Lucy.

"Really, the more I think about the matter, the more sorry I feel for my uncle. When I first realized what was happening, I was bitter toward him, but I'm coming to realize that he's to be pitied rather than scorned."

A slow smile stole over Calvin's features as he went on speaking. "I've always taken for granted, Father, that if I ever had a wife I would relate to her the way you do to Mother. I guess in order for that to be the case, I'd better start now to work harder at relating to women in general the way you do. That will give me a good foundation on which to build a relationship with my wife such as you have with Mother!"

Postscript:

Sadly, when Uncle Elwood was approached by the church concerning his problem, he did not see his need. It was therefore necessary for the congregation to terminate his membership on the grounds that he was not being faithful to his marriage vows and that he was not living in obedience to the Word of God in relation to a husband's care for his wife.

From What I Heard

"FATHER IS TOO PARTICULAR!" Carl fumed inwardly. "He sees some possible inaccuracy in everything I say. He always thinks people might misunderstand me or get the wrong impression. They might unintentionally distort the information I give them when they repeat it. He says that when something is a bit unusual it's often better not to pass it on.

"Well, I'm tired of being reminded that often the things I share with others might better have been kept to myself. And anyhow, had I known he was standing where he could overhear me, I'd never have told the boys about George's new job."

But it was too late to change anything now, for he had told them after church on Sunday morning—told them when Father happened to be standing right behind the door where he was.

"It's the sort of statement rumors grow from, Son," Father told him privately the following morning. "Your problem lies in liking to emphasize the unusual aspects of a matter. The people who hear you don't realize that you're telling them something out of the ordinary, and then they pass the information on as if it were a normal situation. That's why the things you tell people have a way of coming back distorted."

Carl knew that Father was being gentle in his exhortation. Even so, he could not help but feel that his parents were too particular. Why did they have to be so fussy about such little details?

Of course the things he had shared with the boys could be blown out of proportion. But did that mean they would be? After all, he had not said that George would be earning twenty dollars an hour. Nor had he tried to leave the impression that he might be. All he had said was that with contract work, the pay varied from one job to another, and that on one of their recent projects, the men George will be working with each made twenty dollars an hour. He had not said that George would get that much. Why did Father have to be so picky?

. . .

Late that same fall, Carl and his family traveled to

another state to visit relatives. Carl looked forward especially to the three days they planned to spend at Uncle Jerry's. They had several boys near his age, and only one girl, who was several years younger than he was. He hadn't seen any of them for three years.

"Be sure to restrain yourself when you're tempted to share information that won't benefit anyone," Father cautioned Carl as they neared their destination. "You're doing better lately, and I really appreciate that. I just thought I'd mention it since there will be plenty of opportunities for it to happen when you boys are all together."

"Thank you, Father," Carl answered. "I'm sure the reminder isn't out of place."

When the boy cousins were visiting together the following afternoon, Dale, the oldest, shared some of his plans for the future.

"I'll be of age in February," he said, "and since Father doesn't have work for all of us boys here, I've been thinking of going to Bible school this winter. After that I'll get a job somewhere."

"You're probably looking for something close to home," Carl surmised.

His cousin shook his head. "Actually, I've been thinking of going where your brother George is," he said. "From what I've heard, wages are almost unbelievable there. Our sister got a letter from a pen pal of hers, a girl from your congregation, saying that George earns more than twenty dollars an hour. For that kind of money, I wouldn't mind being far away from home..."

Carl did not hear the remainder of Dale's answer. He could feel his face turning red as he searched for words to correct the false impression that had, probably through his own carelessness, been passed on to his cousin. How many more people, he wondered, had been given incorrect information as a direct result of his being too free to share things that would better have been kept to himself?

Did Carl Forget?

"BROTHER PETER, THIS IS Melissa Hunter." The voice on the other end of the connection trembled. "I'm at the hospital in Burgess. Carl has just been admitted. He's really sick!"

"That's too bad, Sister," Bishop Peter answered. "What's his problem? Is there something I can do?"

"Dr. Dane says he has pneumonia." The voice on the other end of the line trembled more than before. "The fast-acting type. And he's had it since yesterday morning. But Thursday is Dr. Dane's day off, so we waited to take him in until this morning. Now he's really sick. Too sick!" Melissa's voice trailed with a muffled sob.

Peter studied the clock on the kitchen wall. It was almost one o'clock already. Several days ago, he had made an appointment for someone to meet him at the church at three-thirty this afternoon. Could he get to the hospital and back before that appointment?

"I'll be there as soon as I can, Sister Melissa. What room is he in?"

Twenty-five minutes later, Brother Peter arrived at the door of the sick man's hospital room.

"Brother Peter! I knew you'd ... come!" Carl reached feebly toward the bishop. "Doctor says ... I'm bad off ... Peter. Oxygen next." Carl gasped for breath after every few words.

From the older man's condition, the bishop supposed that an oxygen tent would certainly be in order. He nodded understandingly. "Let's have prayer before they put you in it."

"You brought ... your satchel?" Carl asked.

"It's in the car. Did you want something from it?"

"Your vial of ... oil is ... in there ... isn't it?"

"Of course," Peter answered. "I'll get it right away!" He had not considered that Carl might ask for anointing, or he would have already had the vial in his pocket. He hustled to the car and back through driving snow. "Lord, it would be so nice if we could have the anointing before Carl is put into the oxygen tent," he prayed as he went.

A few minutes later the simple service had been accomplished. Less than a minute after it was over, the nurse was ready to take her patient to the oxygen tent.

Two days after the anointing, Carl was discharged from the hospital as a well man. Not only his own family and congregation, but also many friends and neighbors rejoiced to see him return. For Carl was one who knew how to make himself small and others large. His day-by-day ministrations, though quiet and mostly unpraised, were a blessing to many.

One afternoon the following February, Bishop Peter's telephone again brought an urgent message.

"It's Melissa, Brother Peter. Carl's sick again, just as he was last year. He's in the hospital now!"

"I'll be right there, Sister Melissa. Thanks for calling." This time Peter slipped the vial of oil into his overcoat pocket before he left the car. He expected to need it, and he was right.

Carl's condition was the same as it had been a year ago. So was his request, and so were the results. Within a few days he was on the go again, though his friends noted sadly that his age showed more than it had before. Carl would surely be missed when God's time came for him to go.

Carl never skipped having pneumonia each winter for the next four years. The illness always struck in February. Each time he asked to be anointed, and each time within a few days he was out of the hospital and attending to his usual errands of mercy.

The seventh winter brought what had become a routine phone call. Bishop Peter dropped what he was doing, vial in hand, and rushed to Carl's bedside again. He visited with the sick man, waiting for the usual request for anointing. But Carl didn't ask.

Brother Peter knew that the nurse would soon come to put Carl into the oxygen tent again. Had he forgotten to ask for the anointing? Or did he think he already had? Finally the bishop felt that he could put it off no longer. "Well, Brother, are you ready for the anointing?" he asked.

The man on the bed shook his head. "No, Brother Peter. Somehow... I don't sense that ... God is ... leading me ... to ask." Carl was silent for a minute, fighting for breath, then he went on. "Each year until ... now I ... felt He wanted ... me to be ... healed. This time ... I don't.

A moment later the nurse entered the room and the visit was over. In the early hours of the following morning, Carl went peacefully home.

Peace on His Terms

"GOTTA SHAVE," BART RAGLAND told himself doggedly. "Boss says I can't come to work like this. Gotta shave." He fumbled with the plug on the electric shaver.

"Gotta get outa here and get me a drink." The familiar getting-up sensations surged through his mind and body. "Yeah. Gotta get outa here and get me a drink."

Finally the shaver buzzed to life. Bart turned toward the mirror, his bloodshot eyes straining to focus on the image in the glass. The shaver wavered uncertainly toward his stubbly face. He was never sure when the metal would touch his flesh.

"Well, Ragland, you've got yourself in a mess!" he addressed the image thickly. The face in the cracked glass stared back at him, sullen, red, and puffy.

It might be different, he thought, if he had grown up not knowing better. But he had been raised by parents who went to church. They had not, however, taken their religion as seriously as they might have, and Bart had not joined the church until he was eighteen.

Maybe, he thought now, it would have been different if he had gotten serious about religion earlier. But he had come to know so much of the world and its ways and had made so many friends among those who lived in sin.

As the shaver wavered back and forth, he thought about the first time he had taken a drink, back when he was seventeen. "Fifteen years ago," he thought bitterly. "It seemed like fun. Even when I was in the army, drink made me feel good. I never dreamed it would lead to this."

He gazed around the room. Unmade bed. Filthy sheets. Dirty windows. Sagging wallpaper. Grimy floor. Smoky ceiling. Littered dresser. Broken mirror. "Home," he reflected sadly. "I call this home!"

"You wouldn't have to," his conscience reminded him. "Dorothy told you again just last month that she wants you to come back. You'd have to quit drinking first, though; she won't accept it."

"I'm going to do it!" he decided. "I can if I want to. It won't be easy, of course. But I've done it before. I can do it again!"

In his excitement he fumbled the shaver and it clattered to the floor. He groped for it, lost his balance, and sprawled on his face. "Yes, Ragland, you've got yourself in quite a mess!"

Bart quit drinking and went home to his wife. He gave up bartending and got a job in a hardware store. He brought all of his pay home. He even went to church.

"I'll go anywhere you want to," Dorothy agreed when Bart told her that he wasn't prepared to attend the church where she had been going while he had been away. "We can work this through together, I'm sure."

"Well, I can't accept anything fanatical," Bart warned. "Take that outfit where you've been attending. All this emphasis on the new birth and holy living is a little too much for me. I never was used to that, you know."

So they found a church that Bart thought met his needs. Dorothy missed the fellowship she had grown accustomed to. But she was desperate to make their marriage work. So she tried to be content in the church Bart chose, even though she felt that it had very little to offer.

Thus it was that Bart had very little support in his new life. After all, no one but Dorothy really cared whether he drank or not. Even the preacher took a glass socially now and then. And within a year of his having quit, Bart was back on the bottle again. A few months later, he was back in the shabby room in a run-down boarding house.

"At least I don't have to listen to Dorothy's nagging," he justified himself. "It's always, 'I'd really like for you to quit again, Bart,' or 'You'd be so much happier if you'd quit for good, Bart,' or 'You have to look ahead; the Judgment is coming and I wish I could feel that you were prepared to meet God.' A man can't listen to that stuff all the time!"

But in his heart, Bart knew that Dorothy hadn't nagged him. He had heard those statements, yes, but only once each, and they had been spread out over several weeks. Deep down, he knew she had been loving and patient with him; that once again the separation was entirely his fault.

One morning the landlady knocked sharply on his door. "Telephone for you, Ragland!"

"Bart." It was Dorothy. He could tell she had been crying. "I want to see you. I want to talk with you. It's really important."

For a moment he almost said, "All right. I'll be over." Almost. But then another voice spoke in the back of his mind: "So ye're gonna let her nag ya agin, huh? Ye're gonna let her tell ya what to do!"

"Nothing doing!" he answered into the receiver. "If you've got something to talk about, say it now!"

"Oh, Bart!" She was crying again. "I'd rather talk face to face. It's been six months, Bart. I want to see you!"

His resolve to be tough melted. "All right," he relented. "I'll come over later."

The account Dorothy gave him of the rehabilitation center for alcoholics did sound convincing. Maybe he would have to give it a thought.

"I made an appointment for you," she concluded.

"You'll have to work along with them, of course. No one can help you if you don't want it."

"I already tried A.A. and it didn't work," he said. "I've quit two or three times on my own, and that didn't work either. I suppose it won't matter if I fail again. So no promises," he concluded. "No promises at all."

The interview with Mr. Ellis from the rehabilitation clinic went well. "I'll have to admit you've got my attention," Bart said. "Maybe you're onto something, I'll think it over."

"Don't spend too long thinking and think yourself out of a good idea," Mr. Ellis responded. "As you said, the worst that could happen is failure, and you're already failing seriously in life. But there's the other side too. You have a wife who still loves you. You'd better think about her. A lot of men in your condition were deserted by their families long ago."

Two months later, Bart had been in the rehabilitation center for several weeks already. It was operated by a church group and there was an appeal made to the patients to surrender their lives to the Lord, primarily as a means of getting help with their alcohol problem.

Bart, however, had tried the church route after having quit on his own, and it hadn't met his needs. So at first he was very leery of the ideas held by the personnel at the center.

As time went on, however, and he saw how patient they were with him and observed how the love of God was making them do the things they did to help others less fortunate than themselves, he began to wonder. At last the day came when he was ready to surrender himself to the Lord, not only for help with his alcohol problem but for forgiveness of his sinful life in all areas.

"I've been exceedingly wicked," he prayed brokenly. "Thank you for showing me how sinful I am. Thank you for sending Jesus to shed His blood on the cross so that I can be forgiven."

By the time his prayer was finished, Bart was a new man. "The Lord has answered Dorothy's prayers," he told Mr. Ellis. "Ever since she's been going to this church she found after I left her the first time, she keeps talking about being born again and giving our lives completely over to the Lordship of Jesus Christ."

"And you hadn't a clue what she was talking about," Mr. Ellis guessed.

Bart nodded. "But now, well, now it all makes such good sense. Why didn't anyone tell me this before?"

Bart knew right away that he had much to learn—much growing to do and many sinful practices to overcome. But there was no question that he who had been dead now lived in Jesus Christ.

He had not had access to alcohol while at the clinic. But as an alcoholic, he knew he could expect a single taste of strong drink to revive his appetite for it. Even the smell of liquor had been too much for him during the months when he had quit on his own.

So he was amazed one evening to find that his job of putting a newcomer at the clinic to bed did not renew his appetite for drink. "He smelled so bad, you'd think he'd been sweating alcohol," Bart told Mr. Ellis the next morning. "But do you know what? I found it repulsive instead of appealing. God has taken even the craving away. I'm so thankful!"

Already on the first day after his conversion, Bart realized that the vulgar language he had become accustomed to using no longer appealed to him. "Lord, take it away completely," he prayed. "I know it doesn't fit with the Christian life. Please, just take those words out of my thoughts."

God honored his request, and although he was occasionally tempted when something did not go according to plan, he soon had victory over the filthy talk he had used for many years.

"I can't do these things on my own, Lord," he prayed. "I can see now that all along I've been trying to—at least when I cared enough to try.

"Show me the other things I need to change too," he went on with his prayer. "I want my entire life arranged according to Your will. I'm under new management, Lord. I've been searching for real peace for many years and never found it. At first, I thought drink was the answer, for at least I could forget my troubles for a while. But now I see it was just the devil's way of keeping me bound in sin."

Several days later, Bart and two other patients at the clinic were cleaning the building. They were expected to work for several hours each day, but they had plenty of spare time too. There was a Bible in each of the rooms, and often Bart would read for a while.

One afternoon before he began to read, he prayed, as usual, "Lord, show me whatever You see in my life that isn't pleasing to You." But this time he felt almost as though God had not heard him.

"I didn't know what to make of it," he told Dorothy later. "I couldn't think of anything I had done that should have caused a problem. But my prayer didn't seem to reach beyond the ceiling. So I talked to Mr. Ellis. He said the Lord wanted me to attend to something I already knew about before He could lead me further."

"Did you know of anything?" she asked.

Bart shook his head. "So I asked the Lord about it, and He reminded me that years ago I had heard one of my uncles say that God doesn't want His children to wear jewelry. Well, I took a look at my wedding ring, and I took a look at my wristwatch with its gold band, and I knew they had to go."

Dorothy studied his hand for a moment, then she slipped the wedding band from her own finger and placed it in his hand. "Oh, Bart," she said. "I've heard that at the church I'm now attending, and just this morning I read about Christians not wearing gold—in the Bible, you know—and I was sure it would include wedding rings, but I just didn't want to give it up. I didn't think you'd understand..." Her voice trailed off, and Bart noticed tears in her eyes.

She pulled the gold watch from her wrist. "You might as well have this too," she added. "It's either now or later."

Bart nodded. "You won't regret this," he promised. "I got rid of my cuff links too. And the shoes with the shiny buckles."

Dorothy looked steadily at him. "Bart," she said slowly, "I think it's time for me to go home and do some housecleaning of my own. We may as well both do this right while we're at it. Maybe our failure to give up this sort of thing in the past caused you to go back to drinking. I never want that to happen again!"

Bart had already thrown his cigarettes and lighter into the incinerator. Now he also discarded a batch of tapes, books, and magazines he knew did not fit with wholehearted service to Christ. "By God's grace," he told Dorothy the next time she came to visit him, "I never want to use any of those things again."

Now, several years later, Bart and Dorothy are members of a church that helps them maintain a close fellowship with the Lord and with other Christians. It also helps them to safeguard their lifestyle and their use of possessions. This church teaches them to relate to the things of this world according to the instructions of the New Testament, realizing that otherwise their possessions could lead them into spiritual danger or even ruin.

"I wanted peace for years," is Bart's testimony now. "But not until I sold out to the Lord completely, allowing Him to do with both me and my possessions exactly as He pleased, did I ever find it. I have learned now that people who want to have peace with God will have to have it on His terms, not on their own."

How Shall He Hear?

He's a man with a soul like you and me,
What though in the gutter he lie?
Yes, a man with a soul like you and me.
Can we casually pass him by?

He's dirty and drunken, despised and alone.
Friend, who will show him the Way?
For he never has seen nor ever known,
And he never has heard us pray.

Is it really so strange that peace he seeks
From a bottle, a shot, or a pill?
For he never has heard of the Way of Life,
And most likely he never will.

I'd Give up Anything!

———◆·◆·◆———

FROM AMONG THE REEDS along the left bank of the river, a bullfrog boomed in the suffocating heat. Frank grinned to himself as he smacked the surface of the water with his paddle and waited for the resulting plop when the frog plunged into the current. A hundred yards in front of the canoe and on the other side of the river, a startled buck instantly began to flail the water in convulsive flight.

"Sorry, fellow," Frank called after him. "I didn't notice you there." The deer had already disappeared into the woods.

"Anyway, I'd better get on to town," he told himself. "The train isn't due for at least three hours yet. But in the meantime Art will be much less miserable in a bed at the hotel than he must be sweltering in the bottom of this canoe."

"How's it going, Buddy?" Frank spoke louder now to get his sick brother's attention. "Does it hurt as much as it did when we left home?"

Art's face contorted and he nodded wordlessly. Three days of intense pain had taken most of the eighteen-year-old's strength. During the twenty-five-mile trip in the canoe, the fever that had gripped him for the last forty-eight hours had increased to near delirium proportions.

The decision to take him to the doctor had been hard to make. Should they wait longer and hope that the pain would leave on its own? Would the trip to the doctor be harder on him than staying at home would be? How would his weakened body respond to twenty-five miles in the canoe and then another two hours by train? That was the only route to medical aid.

Because they had hardly known what to do, they had waited until it became obvious that Art was not going to get well on his own before they set out to find medical attention.

"We'll be at the landing soon," Frank said. "You'll feel better once we get you in a bed." Frank knew, though, that he sounded unconvincing even to himself. At this point, he had begun to wonder whether his brother would ever feel better again. There was no way to put his finger on anything, but somehow the uneasy feeling that Art would not recover kept coming back.

"I'll do my best to see that he makes it!" Frank resolved grimly now. "If only we would know what's wrong with him. Maybe I waited too long to bring him to the doctor. But yesterday the train was going the other way, and the day before that Art was still sure he would get better without any help. If only Father were living, I wouldn't have had to decide."

But Father had been gone for four years now, and Mother had died fourteen years ago, when their brother Harry was born. Frank had been just four then, and Art was barely two.

"Harry," he thought to himself. "How that poor lad needs a father. But all he has is Art and me, Lord. You know how little I can do for him or with him either for that matter. You know how he seems to have no interest at all in spiritual things. Please do whatever it takes to bring him to understand his need of salvation. I'd give up anything You might ask of me if it would cause Harry to see his need of repentance and of giving his life to You. Lord, I want so much to help him find Jesus as his Savior."

The canoe rounded the last bend, and the landing at the edge of the tiny frontier town came into view. Frank secured the canoe to the planks of the dock with a rope and clambered up the bank.

"Stay here," he instructed his brother. "I'll find someone to help carry you to the hotel. You might be two years younger than I, but you're also two sizes bigger. I'll not be gone long."

The village did not have a store. A few houses, a

backwoods hotel, and a hut that passed for a train station—this was a nearly typical eastern Canadian frontier town very early in the twentieth century. One hundred and fifty miles from the nearest city, and fifty miles from the nearest county seat, this backwoods village existed only as a loading and unloading point for the railroad.

The train went out and back on alternate days. It would still be at least three hours before it arrived. Frank hurried to the hotel to seek someone to help transport his suffering brother from the waterfront to a bed.

He was not surprised to find the space behind the counter in the front room of the hotel empty. He had been here before when the only three men who were to be found in the town at this time of day were in one of the rooms further back in the building, playing poker and drinking. The voices back the hall verified his guess; they were there now.

He knocked on the half-open door and stepped inside. The three men at the table ignored him. "Please, fellows," he said quietly, "my brother is terribly sick, and I need help to carry him up here from the dock."

None of the card players looked up. Frank waited until they had finished the hand they were playing. While one of them shuffled the cards, he tried again. "My brother's awfully sick. I need help to get him up here from the landing."

"Look here, Bud! Can't you see we're busy?" one of

the players said coldly. "Your brother's sick. That's hardly our problem, now is it? Why don't you go and bring him up yourself? We're right in the middle of an important game!" The bearded man who had spoken took a long drink from the whiskey bottle at his side before he returned to his cards.

Dumbfounded at their hardheartedness, Frank turned away. "Drink!" he reflected bitterly. "Drink and gambling. Lord, I'm so glad you gave us a father who taught against both." He felt anger welling up within himself to think that they did not care. "Lord, help me feel the way You want me to toward those men. It's not in me to love them on my own."

He trudged back toward the dock. The past two days had been nerve racking, and the miles down the river beneath the July sun had taken their toll on his reserves, even though the current had been in his favor. Now the refusal of the gamblers to help him carry his brother from the canoe to a bed seemed to be the last straw.

"They can't do this to us!" he thought as he turned on his heel and headed back to the hotel. But the memory of their indifference came again to his mind, and he turned back toward the river.

"Give me your hands, Art," he said when he got there. "We'll see if we can get you up here onto the dock." But every attempt Frank made to help his brother move was answered with a groan.

"If only those hoodlums would give me a hand," he

thought. Bitterness swelled in his throat, threatening to choke him. "Lord, I can't live with myself like this," he prayed. "Help me to forgive them as Jesus forgave His tormenters."

Several minutes and much agony later, Art was on his hands and knees on the dock. He could move no further.

"I guess I'll have to carry you," Frank said finally. "There's no other way to get you out of this sun and into the hotel. See if you can sit on this block of wood. I think I can pick you up from there." But Art could move no further.

With a mighty heave Frank lifted the inert form of his brother, the hundred and eighty pounds hanging on his arms like the body of a sleeping child. Would he have the strength to carry such a burden all the way to the hotel?

He had gone only twenty yards when Art stirred. "Put me down, Frank," he said weakly. "The pain just disappeared. I think I can walk now. The Lord must have healed me. Let's go home!"

Nauseating weakness washed over Frank as he slid his feverish brother to the ground. Suddenly he knew what had caused Art's agony. "Oh, no, Lord! Not that! I promised back there on the river that I'd give up anything if it would help Harry find the Savior. But I never thought You might ask me to give up Art! How can You let him die, Lord, when I need him so badly to help me show Harry the way of salvation?"

Frank knew now that he should have guessed that Art had appendicitis. He had heard of it several times. The patient would experience intense pain for several days. Then suddenly the agony would vanish. Two or three days later, the patient would die.

The knowledge seemed more to him than he could bear. "Doubling him up as I did when I picked him up put pressure on the inflamed appendix and it burst. The pain's gone now, all right, but the poison is spreading throughout his body. By the time we reach Dr. Fuller, it'll be too late. Had I had help to carry him up from the landing, this likely wouldn't have happened. Two men together would have carried him flat, not doubled up."

Several hours later, Dr. Fuller examined Art. "I'm afraid you're right, Frank," he said. "From what you've told me, I doubt if there's much we can do. We'll operate, of course, but we probably can't help him. I'll do my best, but I don't want to leave you with false hopes for his recovery."

Gently the two men carried the now unconscious patient to the next room. Frank undressed his brother while the doctor prepared to do the surgery.

Art stirred and opened his eyes for a moment, and they focused on Frank's face. His mouth began to move, and Frank bent low to hear the whispered message.

"Tell Harry ... to meet me ... in heaven." Art slipped into unconsciousness again.

The emotional strain of the past three days brought

Frank to tears at his brother's words, and great sobs tore through him. "Lord, how can I bear this?" he agonized. "My brothers are all I have, and now You're letting Art be taken from me. I want whatever is Your will, but it's so hard, Lord. How can I let him go?"

Two days later, Frank paddled against the current to go home. "Dr. Fuller did everything he could, Harry," he explained to his youngest brother when he arrived. "It was just too late. If only those fellows at the hotel would have helped me. We would have carried him flat, and likely his appendix wouldn't have burst. Maybe then at least he'd have had a chance.

"But the Lord knows all about that too, I'm sure. I'm still struggling with bitterness toward them, though. As far as I can see, it's their fault Art died. Yet he still wouldn't have died even under the conditions he did if God had not allowed it. He always has a purpose for everything."

Frank did not tell Harry about his prayer on the way down the river, for he realized his brother would not understand.

Harry shook his head at the idea that God could have allowed Art to die. "He was too good," he said. "I can't see any purpose in anyone as good as he was having to die so young. All we three boys have had since Father died four years ago has been each other. Now we don't even have Art. I don't see why God would have taken him away from us. It isn't fair!"

"I wouldn't say God took him," Frank replied. "The Lord allowed Art to die, but it's not quite the same as taking him away. Our part now is to accept what has happened as God's will for us. We know Art loved us both." The tears welled up again as Frank relived the last few minutes before Art was given the ether for surgery.

"The last thing he ... said was, 'Tell Harry ... to ... meet me ... in heaven!' " Frank was weeping aloud before he finished the sentence. "Oh, Harry! If only you'd understand how much Art cared about your soul!"

Days and weeks passed, and summer gave way to fall. Still Harry refused to yield his life to God, and still Frank fought with himself over his unforgiving attitude toward the men who had refused to help his brother because their poker game meant more to them than Art's need did.

One crisp September morning, Frank again relived the memories of the events surrounding his brother's death. "I want to accept it as Your will, Father," he prayed. "I want to stop blaming the men who were busy gambling and didn't have time to help us. You know, Lord, that I haven't forgiven them—not the way You forgave me for all my sins. I want deliverance from this bitterness, Lord. I want to love those men the way You love them. Please crucify whatever it is inside of me that wants to see them suffer for what they've done."

He waited before the Lord in silence for a long time then, and gradually the bitterness he had been nursing melted away. In its place, he began to sense a sincere desire that those who had wronged him might somehow find salvation.

"Thank you, Father," he prayed as he realized what had happened. "Continue to search my life now, Lord. Show me anything at all that isn't pleasing to You. And Lord, help me to be a better example to Harry than I've been these past two months. I can see now how foolish I've been, hoping he'd find salvation and at the same time nursing a grudge in my own heart. Forgive me, Father."

A few months after Frank found victory over his bitterness, Harry also found the Lord as his personal Savior, trusting in the shed blood of Jesus for the forgiveness of his sin. Frank and Harry had fifty years to serve the Lord together before Frank was called home. At the time of this writing, Harry is still alive, and is following the Lord's plan for his life.

"Frank's offer to give up anything the Lord might ask of him for the sake of my salvation cost him far more than he ever expected it to," Harry says today. "But it opened the door for me to find Jesus as my personal Savior. And someday I want to make Art's dying wish come true. I'm looking forward to meeting him in heaven by and by."